A WOLF AT THE TABLE

A WOLF AT THE TABLE

A MEMOIR OF MY FATHER

AUGUSTEN BURROUGHS

ST. MARTIN'S PRESS ✹ NEW YORK

Book design by Phil Mazzone

ISBN-13: 978-1-60751-205-9

AUTHOR'S NOTE

Some names have been changed.

For Christopher Schelling, who is short and mean and saved my life and gave me every star that I pointed to. This book belongs to you. Because I never could have written it without your brutish and relentless love. I know I never say it, but I cherish you and love you with all my heart.

ACKNOWLEDGMENTS

I am indebted to Jennifer Enderlin, Tanya Farrell, Frances Coady, John Sargent, Sally Richardson, John Murphy, Christina Harcar, Steve Troha, and everyone at St. Martin's Press and Picador; Haven Kimmel, Robert Rodi, Jeffrey Smith, Timothy Sommer, Lawrence David, Lori Greenberg, Sheila Cobb, Lona Walburn, Jon Pepoon, Suzanne Finnamore, Jill Clayburgh, Dan Peres, Sarah Wynter, Russell Nuce, my Uncle Bob and Aunt Relda, my brother and his family, Judy Robison, and especially Dennis Pilsits, without whom there would be no point. I would also like to thank Paul Sleven and Jonathan Albano for their intrepid support.

In loving memory of George Nicholas Stathakis

A WOLF AT THE TABLE

I F MY FATHER caught me he would cut my neck, so I just kept going. Broken sticks and sharp stones gouged my bare feet, but I didn't consider the sensation. A branch whipped across my face; I felt the sting and for an instant I was fully blind, but I didn't stop.

His flashlight sliced into the woods on either side of me. The beam was like a knife, and I didn't want it on my back. He was out there, behind me somewhere in these woods.

I dashed to the right through a clutch of young silver birch trees and ran up the embankment, crouching to maintain speed. With his bad knee, he would have trouble with the hill. Lumbering forward, he would need to pause and massage the swollen, throbbing kneecap, catch his breath.

When I realized the jabbing slash from his flashlight was gone, I worried that he had cut around and was one step ahead of me. That he was already on the hill, climbing it from the other side. What if I reached the top and he was there waiting?

I veered back to the path, then crossed it. I wanted to pause and listen, but I couldn't. Fear pressed me forward. My breathing roared in my head as though my ears were beside a gigantic heaving machine, a bellows stoking some hellish fire.

Even though I was wearing only pajamas and had no shoes, I wasn't cold. I wasn't anything at all. I was only a blur.

When I stepped on a branch, the rough bark cut deep into my arch, but I just kept going. The pain exploded in my foot and shot out the top of my head, and then was left behind in my wake.

I paused finally and watched the trees for slashes of light but saw none. As my heart settled and my ears became less occupied, I listened and heard nothing but the thready pulse of the night. And I sensed that the hunt was over. Prey knows when it has escaped.

ONE

S ITTING IN MY high chair, I held a saltine cracker up to my eye and peered through one of the tiny holes, astonished that I could see so much through such a small opening. Everything on the other side of the kitchen seemed nearer when viewed through this little window.

The cracker was huge, larger than my hand. And through this pinprick hole I could see the world.

I brought the cracker to my lips, nibbled off the corners, and mashed the rest into a dry, salty dust. I clapped, enchanted.

THE HEM OF my mother's skirt. A wicker lantern that hangs from the ceiling, painting the walls with sliding, breathing shadows. A wooden spoon and the hollow knock as it strikes the interior of a simmering pot. My high chair's cool metal tray and the backs of my legs stuck to the seat. My mother twisting the telephone cord around her fingers, my mouth on the cord, the deeply satisfying sensation of biting the tight, springy loops.

I was one and a half years old.

THESE FRAGMENTS ARE all that remain of my early child-hood. There are no words, just sounds: my mother's breathy humming in my ear, her voice the most familiar thing to me, more known than my own hand. My hand still surprises me at all times; the lines and creases, the way the webbing between my fingers glows red if I hold up my hand to block the sun. My mother's voice is my home and when I am surrounded by her sounds, I sleep.

The thickly slippery feel of my bottle's rubber nipple inside my mouth. The shocking, sudden emptiness that fills me when it's pulled away.

My first whole memory is this: I am on the floor. I am in a room. High above me is my crib, my homebox, my goodcage, but it's up, up, up. High in the air, resting upon stilts. There is a door with a knob like a faceted glass jewel. I have never touched it but I reach for it every time I am lifted.

Above my head is a fist of brightness that stings my eyes. The brightness hangs from a black line.

I am wet-faced and shrieking. I am alone in the awake-pit with the terrible *bright* above my head. I need: my mother, my silky yellow blanket, to be lifted, to be placed back in my box. I am crying but my mother doesn't come to pick me up and this makes me mad and afraid and mad again, so I cry harder.

On the other side of the door, *he* is laughing. *He* is my brother. He's *like* me but he's not me. We're linked somehow and he's home but he's not *home*, like my mother and her voice.

Opposite this door against the wall, there is a dresser with drawers that my mother can open but I cannot, no matter how hard I pull. The scent of baby powder and Desitin stains the air near the dresser. These smells make me want to pee. I don't want to be wet so I stand far away from the dresser.

This is my first whole memory—locked alone in my room with my brother on the other side of the door, laughing.

There is another memory, later. I am in the basement sitting on a mountain of clothing. The washer and dryer are living pets; friendly with rumbling bellies. My mother feeds them clothing. She is lifting away pieces of my mountain, placing them into the mouth of the washer. Gradually, my mountain becomes smaller until I can feel the cool of the cellar floor beneath me.

A form on the wooden stairs. The steps themselves smell sweet and I like to lick them but they are coarse and salty; they don't taste as they smell and this always puzzles me and I lick again, to make sure. The thing on the stairs has no face, no voice. It descends, passes before me. I am silent, curious. I don't know what it is but it lives here, too. It is like a shadow, but thick, somehow important. Sometimes it makes a loud noise and I cover my ears. And sometimes it goes away.

"DID MY FATHER live with us at the farmhouse in Hadley?"

I was in my twenties when I called my mother and asked this question. The farmhouse—white clapboard with black shutters and a slate roof—sat in a brief grassy pasture at the foot of a low mountain range. I could remember looking at it from the car, reaching my fingers out the window to pluck it from the field because it appeared so tiny. I didn't understand why I couldn't grab it, because it was just *right there*.

"Well, of course your father lived with us at the farmhouse. He was teaching at the university. Why would you ask that?"

"Because I can remember you, and I can remember my brother. And I can remember crawling around under the bushes at the red house next door."

"You remember Mrs. Barstow's bushes?" my mother asked in surprise. "But you weren't even two years old."

"I can remember. And the way the bushes felt, how they were very sharp. And there was a little path behind them, against the house. I could crawl under the branches and the dirt was so firm, it was like a floor."

"I'm amazed that you can remember that far back," she said. "Though, I myself can also remember certain things from when I was very little. Sometimes, I just stare at the wall and I'll see Daddy strolling through his pecan orchard before he had to sell it. The way he would crack a nut in his bare hands, then toss those shells over his shoulder and wink like he was Cary Grant."

"So he was there?" I pressed her.

"Was who where?" she said, distracted now. And I could picture her sitting at her small kitchen table, eyes trained on the river and the bridge above it that were just outside her window, the phone all but forgotten in her hand, the mouthpiece drifting away from her lips. "Yes, he was there." And then her voice was clear and bright, as though she'd blinked and realized she was speaking on the phone. "So, you don't remember your father there at all?"

"Just . . . no, not really. Just a little bit of something on the stairs leading to the basement with the washer and dryer and then this vague sense of him that kind of permeated everything."

"Well, he was there," she assured me.

I tried to recall something of him from that time; his face, his hands, his memorable flesh. But there was nothing. Trying to remember was like plowing snow, packing it into a bank. Dense whiteness.

I could remember the pasture in front of the house and standing among rows of corn as tall as trees. I could remember the smell of the sun on my arms and squatting down to select pebbles from the driveway.

I could remember how it felt to rise and rise and rise, higher than I'd ever gone before as my trembling legs continued to unfold and suddenly, I was *standing* and this astounded me and I burst out laughing from the pure joy of it. Just as I threatened to fall on my face, my leg swung forward and landed, and so fast it seemed to happen automatically, my other leg swung forward and I did it again—my first step!—before tumbling forward onto my outstretched hands.

But I could remember nothing of my father.

Until years later, and then I could not forget him no matter how hard I tried.

TWO

BENEATH THE SUN I watched the steps pass quickly between my legs, one after the other after the other. The singularity of the motion hypnotized me as I climbed higher, higher up the Pyramid of the Moon in Mexico.

On the steps below me my mother shouted, "Stop, Augusten! Stop *right now*!" But with my legs scrambling, my hands gripping the step ahead and then pushing it down to meet my feet, the sun so burning white that it filled the entire sky, I'd entered a kind of a trance where nothing existed but the next step. Finally, she was able to catch up and grab me by the ankle.

Breathless, she cried, "My God, why didn't you listen? I was just terrified that you'd trip and fall all the way down."

It was the first time in my life I'd experienced a feeling close to achievement.

I saw that if I continued this strange land-swimming, this intoxicating crawling, climbing, clinging, I would make it to the very top of the world.

I didn't know what a pyramid was. Not once did I consider the consecrated land upon which it was built, or the powerful ancient society that created it. I knew only that it was overwhelming, magnificent, and must be climbed.

My mother waited until I turned five before taking me to Mexico. We'd come with her best friend, Hyacinthe, and Hyacinthe's son, Peter, who was also five. The weeks leading up to the trip had been painful, with repeated visits to the doctor for inoculations.

My mother packed our blue hard plastic American Tourister suitcase with Vienna sausages, which we ate from the can with plastic forks. We drank only bottled Cokes.

During the day we walked through the city, paying for pastries with coins. Clusters of street musicians seemed to follow us. I saw a monkey walking on a leash and thought it was an ugly foreign child. Flags quivered on thin wooden sticks outside cafés, rose petals were strewn on the sidewalk; there were straw sombreros, peeling plaster, and tiny green glass bowls handed out as souvenirs at all the restaurants. Mexico was a swirling blur of color and blast, screaming confusion, and vibrant aromas. Peter and I held hands tightly and charged down the sidewalk, ahead of our bare-legged mothers. We dashed into every store, giggling as we shouted, *"¿Habla usted inglés? ¿Habla usted inglés?"*

In an instant Peter was gone. He'd broken away from me and run ahead on his plump little legs and now his mother cried, "But where did he go? Did you see? Where is my Peter?" We all three turned around and around on the sidewalk, like ballerinas from three different music boxes, looking everywhere but seeing nothing, calling his name and hearing only the sounds of the city in return.

I clung to my mother as we entered stores and asked if

they'd seen a little boy, about my height, my age but with dark hair instead of blond. It was strange, his sudden disappearance, but I accepted it. I expected never to see him again; the hungry city had eaten him. But suddenly his mother spotted him standing beside a *policía* and she ran, screaming, weeping, and waving her arms crazily above her head. I was mystified. In the room that night I'd asked my mother, "But how did she find him? How?" The feeling was like seeing someone step up into the air and fly away. *How?*

My mother held my hand tighter after this, her fingernails biting into my wrist. But she could not protect me.

We visited deep, slick-walled caves, our guide a local man who warned, "People have been lost in these tunnels. Unless you know them very well, it's easy to mistake one passage for another." He wore white and looked like light itself and I followed him faithfully, utterly trusting him.

The tunnels were dark and cool. Somewhere in the center of the cave, he cupped his hands into a black, still body of water and held them out for me to drink, drops falling from his fingers. The water was sweet, so cold it numbed my throat.

Outside, he pulled the needle from a cactus and showed me how, with the fibrous thread still attached, you could stitch a wound if you had to. My mother called me away from him. "Come now," she warned me in a whisper. "We don't really know this man." But he adored me and I knew it. This was a new, euphoric sensation. My first taste of a drug. I wanted more.

Reaching out for his hand, I twisted the silver ring on his thick, hairy finger. He smiled and slipped off the ring, dropped it into my palm. He closed my fingers around it and with his other hand gently stroked my cheek. "I had a boy just your age," he said to me softly as my mother pulled me into step beside her. "Wave good-bye," she said, and I did, turning back to watch him as she led me away. I waved and waved and waved.

In a restaurant, I sat on the chair with my feet tucked beneath me. I wiggled and swung my arms, shrieking, laughing, telling her all I had noticed.

The man had given me his ring and I was happy. It was much too large for my fingers, so my mother kept it in her purse. I continuously watched her bag, as though it might suddenly glow with my ring in its belly.

I was drunk. I was silly and sloppy with joy because the man, who said he'd had a boy my age, loved me and I knew it and felt it and I wanted to go back to him.

The chair tipped. I fell and silently impaled myself through the back on an ornate decorative iron spike attached to the radiator beside me.

Pinned like a butterfly to a setting board, I could not move. I began to cry, growing more afraid as the grown-ups left their tables to gather around me, frantically motioning and shouting in Spanish.

My mother quickly pulled me off the spike and held me against her chest, blood staining her fingers. The manager rushed to the table. He spoke Spanish, she spoke English; language bounced between them, landing nowhere. At last, he drew a map on a napkin and she carried me to the hospital in her arms.

She was relieved, so relieved, to have an American doctor. He told her, "Another inch to the left and he'd have been paralyzed for life."

This memory is vaporous to me now. Dissolved by the medication I was given at the time, it has eroded to almost nothing but her recounting of the story so many years later. "I was just terrified to be in a foreign country, to be in a Mexican hospital. I looked around and felt frantic by how dirty it was."

IN MEXICO MY mother wore thin-soled sandals and looked over her shoulder. She watched me through large, dark sunglasses and said, "We had to get away from your father. He's not safe to be around right now."

This is my first clear memory of my father: I am in Mexico, I am five, and he is not safe to be around.

I could not fathom what this meant. The things I knew that weren't safe included furious dogs, putting a fork in a toaster, rushing water. How was he like these things?

Everywhere we went, an awareness followed us: we were fleeing. The feeling tainted even the food we hastily ate out of the cans stacked in her suitcase, a measure of economy. I was not allowed to have ice because it, too, was unsafe.

WHEN WE RETURNED, we did not go home to the new red house in the woods of Shutesbury. We'd moved into the new red house when I was three. I remember seeing it when it was only wood bones, like the skeleton of a whale. Instead, we went to an apartment in the center of the town of Amherst that I had never seen before. It was on the second floor of a house and had a bay window in the living room, a small kitchen with a cold tile floor. The bathroom had a tub with claw feet and I had my own bedroom. It was just the two of us. My mother sat me on her lap as she explained that my brother was down south with our grandparents, Jack and Carolyn.

But where was my father?

My mother said, "We have to stay here for a while. We can't see your father right now."

Fear wafted from her skin like a fragrance.

"But Mom, why not?"

"Because he's dangerous," she said.

Her words lingered in the room like a third person standing in the corner watching us.

WHEN MY UNCLE Mercer, her brother, came to visit from Cairo, Georgia, he brought me a cardboard box in the shape of a space rocket. He assembled it for me on the living room floor and I crawled inside. But I didn't play with the rocket, I only sat inside and stared at him through the porthole. He had been the first person to hold me after I was born.

At night, he walked me outside to the parking lot so that we could look up. I liked to stare at the night sky. I didn't understand the stars. They looked to me like sparkling lakes, seen from a great distance.

My mother sat on the sofa smoking and whispering urgently to her brother. I didn't listen to her words. But, like a dog, I heard the anxiety and fear in her voice. I sat on the floor and held Mercer's large hand, pulled at his fingers, which were stained yellow and smelled of nicotine. But being in the living room with my wide-eyed and whispering mother made me anxious so I filled the tub with warm water and then climbed inside. I bathed with my new brown plastic Noah's ark, dozens of small animals floating in the water all around me. There were so many new toys that I worried I had traded my father for them. So, except for the Noah's ark, I didn't play with them.

The price for having the ark, I reasoned, was not seeing my father for a while. But to play with all the other toys would be to drive him away for good.

I saw Peter almost every day because my mother spent many afternoons at Hyacinthe's home, an L-shaped one-level ranch just outside town. Peter and I played in the backyard among the skunk cabbage plants that grew in the wetlands behind the house. There were so many cabbages we were compelled to pick them and invent games. One of us would be the shopkeeper, the other the customer. A cabbage cost five round flat stones. We had a wealth of something we didn't want, but the wealth itself was intoxicating and we invented games just so we could experience the sensation of having too much of something.

We watched *Sesame Street* in his basement and we learned to count. We both shrieked with joy when five was the number of the day. We placed olives on each finger and then ate them off, one by one.

Hyacinthe spoke French with her son and I was so jealous of him for being able to talk to his mother in this exotic secret language.

My mother would sit on the sofa and weep while Hyacinthe tried to soothe her, massaging her neck and shoulders and reassuring her in that beautiful, melodious voice. That my mother needed the comfort so frequently, that she wept so constantly, scared me. I felt like we weren't walking on solid ground but on a quivering net suspended in the air, and at any moment our feet could plunge through the holes.

I learned to ride a bike in the parking lot of our new apartment house. Now six years old, I was enrolled in Wildwood Elementary School. Because my mother had told me our living situation was "temporary" and that eventually we would be reunited with my father and move back into our red Shutesbury house, I found that I could not concentrate in school. I avoided making friends because I would just have to give them up eventually. But my reluctance was misinterpreted by the other children and I became the object of bullying. The defining moment occurred on the playground one afternoon when my class divided into two groups, the boys and the girls, with each group chanting at the other, "boys are better than girls," and "girls are better than boys." I stood between the two groups, trying to remain neutral. "Come on," one of the boys shouted at me. "Come over here." But I joined the girls instead, since they seemed less hateful and were certainly much cleaner than the boys. "Girls are better than boys," I sang out, the only one on my side of the playground without a barrette or a hair band.

From then on I was despised by the girls *and* the boys. The boys hated me for siding with the girls, for virtually becoming one before their eyes. And the girls plain mistrusted me.

I became the sickly kid. Some mornings I ran a high temperature or displayed a rash of raised, red bumps. Other days my malady was more amorphous; I just didn't *feel* good. I saw the doctor more frequently than my mother could afford. She worried about money, standing in front of the phone, biting her lip, knowing she had to call my father to ask for more but unable to do it. I missed a lot of school. Some mornings, just imagining the blue metal doors of the building caused my stomach to clench miserably. I only wanted to stay home in bed; home with my mother, grilled cheese sandwiches, and Fanta orange soda.

My mother drove a brand-new, 1971 red Chevy Vega, which she named Rosie. It had a black interior and a manual transmission, and the small car smelled new inside. Each day when I saw it pull into the parking lot, I nearly wept with relief. Opening the heavy passenger door, I climbed inside and slid onto the vinyl seat.

"How was school?" my mother asked.

"I just want to go home."

Some days, my mother was bright and hopeful, her hair washed and her spirits high. "Would you like to drive to Northampton and go to the Farm Shop for a Golden Abigail?" The cheeseburger with crinkle-cut french fries, served in a red plastic basket, was a favorite meal.

But other days she arrived disheveled, with creases from the pillow etched into the soft skin along the side of her face, like a tree bare of leaves. Her hair was oily and unkempt and she was despondent, her eyes ringed with red. On these days, she worried out loud, "I'm just afraid that if we go back home to your father that something terrible will happen but I don't know how much longer we can survive on our own." Her hands trembled, even as she gripped the steering wheel.

But I missed his presence, the fact of him in the house. And I didn't understand what had happened. Why, suddenly, was she afraid? Why was he dangerous? Why hadn't he come with us to Mexico? And why were we living in this strange, small apartment when we had a brand-new home?

So much had happened since I last saw my father that I wasn't even the same person anymore. At night when I was supposed to be sleeping, I'd lie awake and wonder if he would like the new me. And I was new, wasn't I? Didn't every new thing you did become a part of you, one of your bricks? I was part Mexico now, and part new school, and part bicycle with no training wheels.

My mother said he was sick. I asked, "Is he in the hospital?" Standing at the dingy, chipped porcelain sink in the small kitchen and arranging wildflowers in a rinsed-out jelly jar she said, "Not that kind of sick." She wouldn't look at me.

I wanted to bring him my hot water bottle. It always made my stomach feel better. I knew I might need it myself, but I would give it up for him, I really would. She kissed the top of my head and said, "We'll see."

AT NIGHT MY mother locked the door and checked the windows. She picked up the telephone to check for a dial tone. She made sure we had candles and matches, as if we were preparing for a huge storm, the certain failure of our electricity. Her fear leeched into me, became mine. My father, already a mysterious man I used to see mostly at night when he came home from work, became a larger and more ominous presence in my life. Though I could no longer form an image of his face in my mind, I felt him under my bed, behind the closed door to my closet, lurking in the shadowed corners of our small, temporary home. I started to fear him instead of miss him. If he'd suddenly appeared at the front door, I might have shrieked and run in the opposite direction.

I BEGAN VIOLIN lessons with a private instructor. Once a week, I was taught how to tuck the instrument under my chin, curling my thumb against the underside of the neck. Over and over, I raked the bow across the strings, trying to achieve a sound and not a screech. I learned the names of its various components: the frog, the bridge, the tailpiece, and the pegs. And while I was proud to be able to name the parts of its anatomy, it was the smell of wood, rosin, and velvet that I loved. The best part of every lesson was opening the violin case and lowering my face to inhale. Also, it seemed almost a miracle to me that this hollow figure eight, as light and elegant as a lady, as my aunt Curtis, was made from wood, from a tree, like the trees out back behind our house in Shutesbury. I just could not see how this was even possible. And that wood—*wood*—could make a sound so ethereal you were tempted to look over your shoulder and see if somebody transparent were standing right behind you, watching and smiling. It gave me that looking-at-the-night-sky feeling. It made me think of the word *God*.

I longed for my father to see me holding such a beautiful thing so properly; it seemed impossible that so massive an addition to my life could occur without his knowledge. And then I felt guilty for thinking of him and betraying my mother. By longing for him, it was like I was inviting him back into our lives. And if I was inviting him back when my mother was so afraid of him, I was responsible for scaring her. And her trembling and weeping—it was my fault.

I destroyed the violin by winding the strings so tight the neck snapped.

My mother wasn't angry with me. She sat me down and told me it was natural to feel upset and angry with my father. I hadn't known I was angry with him, but because she said I was I began to wonder if it was true.

Soon, I couldn't remember why I'd ruined the violin and could no longer play it. I'd only wanted to see him without hurting my mother, but she'd said I was angry with him, and I had broken my instrument's neck, so maybe it was true.

Nothing made sense to me anymore. I knew I was young, I knew I was small. But I was worried that I might already be ruined.

• • •

IN TIME, I began to feel I had no father. When I made friends
with a girl my own age, it was our mutual fatherless status that
bonded us. Tina's father lived in China, which was so far away I
could not conceive of it, as incomprehensible as if he lived in
the year 1600. For her birthday, Tina's mother baked a red velvet cake and although I declined a slice, feeling too anxious to
eat in front of strangers, I would think about that cake for years.
I'd never seen red cake before. What was wrong with me that I
would decline it? All the other kids had accepted a slice. Why
hadn't I? Why had my stomach been wrenched into an impossible knot? Why was I filled with dread at the prospect of being
seen consuming it? When I thought about this some more, I realized it was not the cake that upset me, but the community surrounding the cake. It was the other kids. I knew they'd end up
teasing me and I didn't want to have a mouth full of cake when
one of them finally reached out and punched me in the stomach, which I was sure would happen. Better to refuse the cake
and be allowed to sit alone, apart from the table. Better, always,
to be self-contained.

Shortly after this party my mother announced that we were
moving back home to live with my father. There was no transi-
tion, because the house was packed and the boxes were moved
while I was at school. One day, we were simply home again.

My father greeted us without any fanfare. He patted me on
the head three times and stiffly hugged my mother but she
pulled away. Then he sat in the living room and watched TV. He
didn't even notice that I was taller and bigger on the inside. And
it was as if none of it had happened: the violin and that strange
school where I never fit in, my friend with a father in China, the
red velvet cake.

Back home, I rode my new bike down the driveway but

tumbled off and scraped my knee. My father bolted the training wheels back onto the bike, which made my face turn deep red with shame. "You just weren't ready," he explained.

Except I had been ready. I'd been riding for weeks without training wheels, and if only he'd seen me he would know this. "I don't need them, really!" I cried, but he installed them anyway, wrenching the bolts on hopelessly tight.

I was desperate to show him what I could do on my own. But my father, because he hadn't been there, simply didn't believe what I was actually capable of accomplishing.

THREE

THE COLD WOOD floor in my bedroom was always a bit of a shock in the morning, a spank to the soles of my feet that made me hop onto the square of carpet in the center of my room. There, I sat down and put on my socks, remembering my aunt Curtis had taught me how to get my heel in the right place. She'd flown up from Georgia the winter my mother and I had moved back into the Shutesbury house and even though I was pretty old now, seven, I still saw her showing me how to line up the heel of the sock with my foot. I also remained convinced that she peed through her panty hose, because I'd seen her sit on the toilet and pee and it didn't look like she pulled down her hose at all. She insisted that she most certainly did and merely hadn't pulled her hose down *all the way*, because I was standing right there watching her.

After my socks, I put on my green jeans, which I insisted on wearing because of Mr. Green Jeans, who was Captain Kangaroo's sidekick. Green jeans, I was almost certain, possessed some sort of rare power. And while I wasn't yet sure what this power was and what it would enable me to do, I knew I would eventually find out. I suspected I might be able to fly when wearing them, but hadn't had the opportunity yet to test this theory. I slipped on a turtleneck, laughing when my head became stuck in the turtle part. If they weren't called turtlenecks, I wouldn't have worn them.

Skidding into the hallway, I clutched the door frame and looped around to the door right next to mine and opened it. In the dark, I saw a hulking form beneath the covers. And then there was the stench that accompanied it. I didn't much like him but he was mine so I turned on the light. "Get up, get up, get up."

Eight years older, John Elder, named for the "Elder" side of the family, was my Big Brother. Big and awful is more like it. Big and stinky, big and greasy, big and dumb. One time he tricked me into looking inside this big hole he'd dug in the yard, and then he knocked me over into it headfirst and started to bury me with only my legs sticking out. My hatred for him nearly caused my skin to steam, and I was constantly plotting revenge for one thing or another.

The other thing was that I'd experienced some confusion about him, because first we went to Mexico without him, and then my mother and I lived in the little Amherst apartment without him. So was he temporary, on loan from some other family? But my mother said, "Of course he's your big brother. He always has been, he always will be. John Elder used to hold you when you were a baby."

"He did?" I was horrified that she would let him hold a baby, prone as he was to either dropping or throwing things, if not plugging them into electrical outlets just to see what would happen.

But now we were back in the same house together, I guessed, forever.

"Quit it, varmint," he hollered. "Turn off the light."

"But it snowed," I told him. "Come on, it snowed."

He liked the snow as much as I did. It created an immediate truce to any and all ongoing wars. He threw off the covers, grabbed his thick glasses and shoved them onto his greasy face, then followed me down the hall to the closet.

We both had snowsuits, blue. We put them on side by side in the front hall near the door. And while he seemed to have no trouble at all, I kept getting caught up in the legs, then I couldn't work the zippers. By the time I finally managed to get myself inside the thing, I was so hot that I was sweating and only wanted to rip it off. My arms stuck out from my sides and I had to walk stiff-legged. To get down the stairs I had to slide on my stomach feet first, using my hands as brakes.

When we entered the basement my brother said, "Watch that furnace. It eats small children like you."

"It does not," I said, believing not one word out of his mouth but keeping my distance from the furnace nonetheless.

We opened the door to the backyard and white light filled the room.

Side by side, we stood wordlessly in the doorway, just looking out at the yard blanketed by so much impossible white. It was wondrous. Snow clung to the limbs, and they sagged under the weight of it. Even the slenderest finger of a branch was piled high with white and I stopped breathing without realizing it, because just my breath might disturb the tenuously balanced snow. For a moment, the world was perfectly still and clean and miraculous.

"You go first," I said.

He hesitated.

We were both afraid to dent the perfection of the white.

"On the count of three. Ready? One, two . . ." And we leaped, together. "Three!" we shouted, the word expelled from our lungs by the force of our landing. I'd plunged chest-deep into the drift in front of the door and now I couldn't stop laughing. The temptation to throw my body around the yard and sink into the snow was nearly irresistible. No longer were there any rocks, sticks, or snakes back here. There was just this icy fluff everywhere. Magic protection.

WITH SHOVELS WE dug a network of tunnels deep enough so that we could crawl throughout the yard, invisible. "You still there?" we called out to each other, just our disembodied voices floating over white.

LATER, OUR MOTHER stood on the deck above us. She sipped her black coffee from a mug with the Morton salt girl printed on the side. Her red bathrobe was knotted at the waist, the bow tied with only one loop. "Where are my boys? Where have they gone?" she called, pretending not to see us in our tunnels.

Both of us crawled to our nearest exit, popped our heads up like prairie dogs and looked at each other, thrilled and surprised by the distance we'd made. The tunnels really *were* as long and winding as they felt.

And then a few moments later she appeared at the basement door holding our father's camera. "Here, now," she said. "Why don't you boys crawl down into this tunnel right here, then poke your heads out and let me get a picture." She fiddled with the dials on the silver and black camera, the strap looped around her neck.

Years later, I stared at this photograph, mesmerized, disbelieving. But there it was: proof that my brother and I had grown up together in the same house, evidence that we were brothers, that we had been a pair at one point in time.

I was so happy.

In the picture, you can see it: my snowsuit, the sun behind me, my happiness.

As we expanded our tunnels, connected them, built emergency exits, the driveway was being plowed by Mr. Sheffield, my school bus driver.

Later, our father came outside to shovel the front steps and all the way down to the driveway. My brother joined him and the two of them scraped their shovels to the bare gravel.

I was too small to do any useful shoveling. I watched.

Watching them work together like this, I understood that they had some kind of *something* together. My brother had been born before me so of course he had been a part of my father's life for longer. Normally, I never thought about those extra years they had lived together as a family. *The family* hadn't really begun, I assumed, until I was born. But I was wrong and the proof was just before me, two shovels in hand, a bank of snow growing larger.

I LOVED LIVING in the red house in the woods, with its black deck that was surrounded on all sides by those towering pines. There were always birds on the branches, small gray birds with dark little apple-seed eyes. They were skittish things that twitched and moved jerkily. Standing on the deck and looking in any direction, you always sensed movement but couldn't quite see where it was coming from. It was peaceful. And with the large sliding glass doors to the deck open, an actual wind would blow all through the house, one of my mother's operas on the record player blending with the breeze so that the dramatic high notes could make your hair blow around.

My parents saw their psychiatrist together in Northampton on Saturdays. Sometimes, they saw him more than just once a week. I felt insulated, protected.

Mexico and that strange, lonely apartment seemed so far away. I had my big brother and I had my mother. I had tuna melts on Roman Meal bread and a fireplace. Best of all we had three dogs. Cream was a smooth-coated, pale tan golden retriever mix. She was clever and would ring the doorbell when she wanted to come inside. Also, she knew she wasn't allowed on the couch and when we came home, there she'd be, sleeping curled up next to the door. But when you went over to the sofa and put your hand on the indentation of the cushion, it was warm.

Brutus was a black and tan rottweiler, fearless and bold. My uncle Mercer had sent him up from Georgia because he was worried he'd be hit by a car on Mercer's busy street. He wasn't as smart as Cream, but he had his charms, acting as my bodyguard when I played my Arriving at the Oscars! game outside, using the blue wheelbarrow as my limousine.

And last, there was Grover, a little black elkhound with a curlicue tail. Grover, unlike the other dogs, wasn't allowed inside. He was christened our "outdoor" dog by my father and he practically never left the deck where he slept, pressed against the sliding glass doors.

It upset me that one of our dogs wasn't allowed inside, and

for no reason that I could understand. Because his coat was long? Because he was smaller than the other dogs? It didn't make any sense to me and when I asked my father, "Why can't Grover come inside?" he always replied, "Because Grover is an outside dog." Like there was a special breed of dog that might die if exposed to a sofa.

Even on the coldest winter night when Grover was no more than a black, furry mound curled into himself and pressed up against the house, my father wouldn't let him in.

Sometimes, I let bad thoughts linger. Like, if my father made Grover sleep outside in the cold, what stopped him from locking *me* out there, too? He had two sons; what if he decided to make the younger one the "outside" son?

I WAS ALWAYS excited when my mother went shopping for fabric and patterns because I loved the smell of the drawers where the patterns were kept at the stores. It was a sweet, clean smell, unlike anything else and it was the same at every store. She bought patterns for dresses, curtains, tablecloths, vests, and skirts. Then she sat for hours at her black sewing machine, her big toe working the foot pedal, a row of needles between her lips. Every few minutes she would reach up and take one of these needles, insert it into the fabric. I wanted desperately to touch the smooth, warm machine. But she almost never let me touch it, worried the needle would stitch my fingers. It never crossed my mind that the sewing machine was not a pet with feelings, needs, and desires. I could not fathom why she hadn't given it a name and I suggested many names, often pinching her on the arm so she would finally look at me so that I could say, "Well, what about Penny? That's a good name."

Tuna melts, my treasured dogs, my mother's nameless sewing machine pet—I loved all of these home things. And the thick, tarry scent of the railroad ties that formed the steps leading to the concrete stairs of the house. The deep, shag carpeting in the living room, which would be like a huge forest if you were small enough to walk around inside of it.

Most of all, I loved my father.

He was rare and extraordinary because I seldom saw him. He was always at his university, being a teacher, so when he came home, it was the biggest event of my day—unless I'd been able to find money in the sofa cushions or in the pockets of one of the coats hanging in the closet.

Hours before he was due I would begin asking my mother, "When will he be home? Is he almost here? How much longer?" I patrolled the house, walking from the living room to the dining room, through the kitchen and into the foyer, down the hall. I checked each bedroom before going downstairs, where I searched my parents' bedroom and the basement, even under the stairs. I had to make sure he hadn't come home without my notice, that he wasn't hiding somewhere.

As I walked through the house, I touched his things. The gray metal lockbox where he stored monthly bills, his badger hair shaving brush, and a gold Hamilton pocket watch he never carried but always wound. I touched my tongue to the antenna of his black shortwave radio, which was centered on the kitchen table. As I expected, it had no taste. Only metals like brass and bronze really had much of a flavor, I'd found.

If I woke up in the middle of the night to get a drink of water, I often found my father sitting at the table, carefully rotating the radio dial to fine-tune a signal from China, or somewhere in the Caribbean.

He wrote to the stations that he reached, brief notes to let them know he'd picked up their distant signal, all the way out in little Massachusetts. As was their custom, they sent him in return a notice called a "QSL card." *Greetings from Northern Ireland. Thank you for listening to the South African Broadcasting Corporation.*

"Imagine that," he'd say, turning the card over in his hand, one side an illustration of a radio antenna superimposed over the Kremlin, the other filled with exotic letters, characters I could not decipher, and the station's call sign. "This very card came from somebody all the way on the other side of the world. Just imagine that, will you?"

I was not allowed to touch the cards—he wanted to preserve the fact that a foreigner had touched them before he had. I understood his thinking. And looked forward to a day in the future when we would pull out the cards and touch them all, all at once. It would be like touching the fingers of people all over the world. A very special occasion.

I felt very close to my father examining his things. In a way, he *was* his things.

Sometimes, I lined a few articles in a row—a pack of his cigarettes, his leather coin purse, the round cork coaster he always used—then leaned over to pass my nose across each item, as though conducting my own olfactory orchestra, the different scents blending to create him whole before me, whenever I wanted.

After the last of the terrible, stubborn sunlight was drained from the sky it was finally dark, my favorite time. I stood in the living room in front of the sliding glass doors that overlooked our driveway. There were no lights along our narrow dirt road and trees packed both sides, making it feel more like a tunnel than a street. Cars could be seen well in advance as their headlights struck the silvery trunks of the pine trees. My eyes could be fooled into seeing the light as somebody running in the woods, their white shirt disappearing behind a tree, reappearing on the other side.

Past six o'clock, cars crackled steadily down our quiet dirt road—professors in Volvos and Saabs heading home. Nearly every house nearby contained a professor. But only one of the cars was my father's gold Chrysler New Yorker, a gift from his parents in Georgia. This would soon be replaced by a dour brown Dodge Aspen wagon so bare of features it didn't even have an AM radio, just a blank metal panel where a radio should be, like an automotive birth defect.

"My father's home!" I screamed, wild with pent-up anticipation and sugar from the raw cake batter I'd eaten earlier.

And I ran, sliding over the wood floors and knocking against the walls. "My father's home!"

It was just so thrilling. He was the missing piece, restored. The king in a game of chess.

As soon as he opened the door, I was on him. In the winter, his hands were icy cold and they made me scream with joy as they touched my face—freezing!—pushing me back. I tried to climb him like a tree. Fighting against his arms, those tricky arms, I had to get around them because they always tried to stop me. "Stop, stop, stop," he'd say, the arms blocking my way to *him*.

I pulled on the hem of his jacket, his sleeve. I grabbed his cold fingers and yanked them. I said, "Pick me up, pick me up!" Melting snow fell from his cap onto my neck and slid down my back, and this made me screech and laugh and jump in place. My father winced and complained, "Hush, that sound hurts my ears."

"Pick me up!" He never did, but I said it anyway.

"Damn it, son, please."

I backed away, still fidgeting and twitching with excitement. "Okay," I said, and allowed him to walk into the house unmolested. Was he heading for the kitchen? Or the living room? I ran ahead of him, tearing across the floor. I made it to his destination long before he did. I hopped in place, up and down, up and down. I just could not stand it!

Finally, when he reached the kitchen or the dining room table, I hugged him. And then those arms of his slid down between us, prying me away.

It made me giggle. "You're tickling me," I shouted.

I always managed to hang on for a little bit longer.

I always won!

It was our game and I loved it. Me against the armsandhands to get to him, his solid core part, the middle, the *him*.

Plus, I had so much to show him. There were drawings for one thing. And sometimes at school I made something out of flour clay and I had to show him this, too. Or my room, my room! I almost forgot, I moved everything around and he had to come see it *right now.*

But he wanted his bottle. The bottle was his and it was important and not to be touched, but I touched it anyway.

He belonged to my mother the most and I knew it. "Let me speak with your father for a while. You can have him later," she'd say. Then I knew I had to go away, so I trotted back to my room and waited and waited and waited.

I'd get to see him again at dinner. He sat at one end of the table, my mother sat at the other. My brother and I were on the sides and my brother read while we ate.

I had an awful lot to say but my mother raised her hand like she was directing traffic. "This is our time." So I had to listen and eat, listen and eat, listen and eat. Sit, sit, sit. I hated to sit but what could I do? I smiled and chewed, chattered softly to myself. I bounced just enough to attract a narrow, warning glance from my mother and then I stopped right now this instant. I smiled, showing my teeth. She looked away, weary. She might have been mad at me because earlier she had let me lick an envelope and it was good so I went into her study and licked all the envelopes in the box.

And then it was bedtime and I had to be alone. I hated bedtime. I could hear them in the kitchen. I could see the warm light crawling in under my door. My brother got to stay up later. But I had to stay flat and sleep. It was just horribly unfair because after dinner he should have been mine. She should have shared. *Not fair.*

After I was settled in bed, my father stepped into my room. "Good night, son."

I replied, "Good night. I love you," my voice rising to an invitation.

"I love you, too," he said, from habit.

He backed out of my room. "Very much I love you," I said, smiling because I knew just what would happen next. This had been our routine for most of my seven years.

"Very much I love you," he answered mechanically, closing the door.

That was it. We spoke those words every night, just like that. The door would not be opened again until the morning.

On the weekends, he was home all day. I could have him. And this is what I thought about before I fell asleep. The whole, fat weekend just around the corner. My father, my father, my father.

Presents!

It was my first thought when I woke up the next morning and dressed for school. Maybe if I brought my father presents when he walked in the door at the end of the day, he might be happy to see me, as happy as I was to see him. At least his tricky arms would be busy and I could get to him.

Late that afternoon, I begged my mother to take me to Hastings, the store in downtown Amherst where you could buy pens and glue and construction paper and model airplanes and Matchbox cars. I wanted nearly everything, though I was only there to buy crisp, large sheets of white paper. The worn, wood floors and walls with paint peeling in strips like sunburned skin somehow made me want everything even more. They had a balsa wood airplane with clear, plastic wings that I would trade my brother's life for. But I stayed focused. Only paper, only paper!

I took the paper home and with my mother's scissors, cut words from magazines.

Love. Belong. New. Exciting. Delicious. Father. Together. Happy. Welcome home!

I pasted these words to the paper and connected the words with a Magic Marker line. I drew a small picture of myself, a larger image of my father.

When he came home, I barreled into him, slamming the collage against his stomach.

To my astonishment, my father was *mad*. And his hands, instead of being busy with the card like I'd planned, came directly at *me* and swatted. Smack, smack, smack. He slapped my shoulder.

My mother had to tell him, "John, he *made* that card for you." These were the words that suddenly made him stop hitting me. And all of a sudden, he was not mad anymore. It just drained away exactly like water from a sink, leaving behind not one drop. And he took the drawing and said, "Oh, that's very good."

The sudden change stunned me more than the slapping had. Plus, I could tell he thought the card was dumb. My mother made him like it, that's all.

When the dog came up to him he reached down and stroked her on the back. I stood back and watched this, dumbfounded.

"Yes," he said, in a much kinder tone than he ever used with me, "you're a good, good dog." He scratched behind her ears.

It wasn't fair because, the dog didn't even know. She hadn't waited all day like I had. She just slept. She didn't even care. It was so unfair.

But it got me thinking.

And the next time he opened the door, home from work, I met him with black construction paper ears, a black construction paper nose, a black construction paper tail, which he couldn't even see.

When he walked through the door it took him a moment to notice that there was something different about me, something paper and canine. And then he complained, "What's that mess on your face, son?"

I turned right there and scampered away from him on my hands and knees then sat in the kitchen, beneath the table. I lapped water from the dogs' bowl and curled up in Cream's spot near the sofa.

I realized that I enjoyed the view of the house from this perspective. It was entirely new.

It was like living in a new house. I saw the undersides of tables, walked through the tangle of chair legs. It would be good to be a dog, I thought. You would feel safe surrounded by all of these leggy objects that never tried to run away.

I wore the ears and nose and tail while I sat at the kitchen table and my mother took a picture of me.

I didn't smile. My mother thought having my picture taken would cheer me up. It usually did. Cameras seemed to have a druglike effect on me, greatly improving my mood on the spot. But I was sad because I was losing against the Arms. No matter what I did, I couldn't get past them and get to my father. They were always in the way, busy swatting and batting.

He shuffled painfully into the dining room, placing his black briefcase on the teak dining table. Then he walked like always over to the credenza, also teak, and poured himself a drink, filling the glass all the way to the top.

I crawled into the room and reached above my head for the briefcase on the table. I unsnapped the clasps and opened it. I hunted with my fingers for the Certs breath mints that I knew were there. Usually spearmint but sometimes he carried blood-red cinnamon Certs, which tasted to me like Lavoris mouthwash and were, therefore, entirely irresistible. But after my father watched a news report about the dangers of red dye number two he stopped buying cinnamon Certs and Lavoris and everything red, saying they would give us cancer. But my mother continued to chew her slender sticks of red Trident gum. My mother did not trust Walter Cronkite. My mother trusted only her psychiatrist.

Until now, I'd always assumed the Certs were something special, just for me. A little surprise my father brought home, to make me happy. So when I discovered that the pack was already opened, a mint or two missing, it puzzled me. Normally, I would take the mints and eat them all and the next day, there would be more. And now, some were missing.

It dawned on me then that they had never been a treat just

for me. They were *not a little surprise* my father brought home just for me. They were his mints and I ate them so he had to constantly buy more.

I understood that instead of being a treat for me, the Certs had been a mild compromise for him. By letting me believe they were a special something, just for me, he didn't have to actually think of a special something just for me.

I sat there on the rug and looked at my father's legs as he strode across the room to take his position in the rocking chair to watch the evening news.

Maybe it shouldn't matter to me why he bought the mints, I thought. *Mints are mints, who cares why he buys them?*

But I did care. The truth was, I didn't really like mints. I only loved these mints because he brought them home for me. But he hadn't given them, I had taken them. To me, this difference was enormous, the largest thing I could imagine.

A couple of mints had shifted the axis of my world.

FOUR

I WAS MESMERIZED by the old black-and-white photographs of my father when he was young. Some were in leather albums, affixed to the page by small black tabs at the corners of each picture. Others were matted and framed, but no longer appreciated, stacked against the rear wall of a closet behind raincoats, jackets, a row of winter boots with the white dust of road salt dried on their soles. But most of the photos were stored loose in a Gilbey's gin box in the basement next to the oil tank. I was consumed for hours, examining each image, trying desperately to feel in my chest, to truly believe, that the boy astride the racehorse and the boy standing in front of the marble-topped soda fountain in the old-fashioned drugstore was my own father when he was young.

My father was in the center of every frame. In one, a wood-paneled station wagon with the liftgate down was parked on the sand, the ocean shimmering behind it, and my father standing in the foreground wearing knickers and a handsome blazer, his smile broad and confident. In another, a rolling pasture was bordered by a white fence that seemed to extend forever, following the gentle curve of the low hills as faithfully as a finger tracing the contours of a body. A chiseled horse, its coat so glossy it reflected the sun as a misty white flair, was half out of the frame, incidental. The camera only cared about the small boy off beside the horse, the sailor in miniature examining a stalk of grass between his fingers.

"That is my father," I told myself, speaking the words aloud so they would exist in the world and begin to become real. But I didn't believe them. It was easier to imagine that this boy the lens admired was not my old, rotten-toothed father, but my secret brother, dead from consumption or given away to live with a movie star, and replaced with me.

"I was just about the same age you are now," my father said when I asked him about the photos. I bit my bottom lip, sucked it into my mouth, and delicately nibbled the skin. I looked at his crispy fingers, ruined by psoriasis, the corner of the photo pinched between his gruesome thumb and forefinger. It was as if he were telling me that he'd once had a tail.

"Why are you standing in a drugstore?" I asked, pointing to another image.

A smile formed on his face, something like pleasure flickering behind his lashes. He leaned back, gripped the arms of the chair with his hands. "My grandfather Dandy, that would be your great-grandfather, he owned that drugstore, right there in downtown Chickamauga. And every Saturday, I would spend the day in there, making ice cream sodas behind the counter, reading comic books. Sometimes, he'd let me ring something up on the old cash register. . . ."

I sat at my father's feet and stared up at his face but he wasn't looking at me. He was gazing off into the distance, peering into the past, seeing people and places decades out of my line of sight. As he spoke, I studied his face, his hands, and I felt a black ball of dread begin to form in my stomach. Was I going to look like him when I grew up? Would my teeth rot in my mouth, just like his? Would my skin peel off and leave those patchy areas of raw meat? After all, if that boy in the pictures really was my father, he started off looking an awful lot like me. I desperately wanted to ask him, *When I grow up, am I going to turn into you?* but I didn't dare. And I wouldn't think about it anymore, either. If you pondered some things, even for an instant, they might become real.

MY FATHER WAS born in 1935 to two teenagers, Jack and Carolyn, in Chickamauga, Georgia. Carolyn was fifteen, Jack seventeen. When Carolyn gave birth, her father, Dandy, thought it was a real shame for such a young couple to be saddled with a baby, waking up every three hours to feed it, their own lives forfeited for diaper changes and burping. They deserved some time alone together to just be married and grow up.

Which is how my father came to spend his first seven years with his granddaddy Dandy, and three teenage aunts, Marjorie, Betty, and Dixie the Baby, who was referred to as Dixie the Baby until the day she died at eighty-one.

Dandy's good nature served him well as the town's druggist, but raising racehorses was his passion. Racehorses and daughters, that is.

The aunts were nearly mad with joy over suddenly having a boy in the house. They spoiled him wickedly, giving him the first, best bite of their own desserts, always spooning an extra dollop of whipped cream into his hot chocolate, making sure he was on the other end of every wishbone at Thanksgiving. When he scraped his knee, all three fussed over him, "Oh, *precious*," and bandaged the wound as though attending to the rituals of a religious ceremony.

The sisters led him to his bedroom at night, peeling back the ironed ivory-colored sheets from his twin mattress and bribing him under the covers with the promise of a story. Sitting on the bed, the girls, dressed in satin nightgowns of pink, mint green, and blue as pale as a vein, passed around his favorite book, *The Velveteen Rabbit,* and read it out loud. Then, one by one, they filed from the room, but not before bowing their heads, as if in prayer, to softly kiss his forehead.

My father was an adored pet boy who was never allowed to suffer one moment's discomfort. He was never required to wait more than an instant for anything, not when there were three vigorous girls in the house, bouncing on the balls of their feet in eagerness to serve him.

The sisters gathered around him in a clutch and sat him at their skirted dressing table, easing his resistance. "It's okay, honey, we just want to see how you'd look." Their clear, blue eyes gleamed with mischief.

They dipped their fingers into the rouge and smeared it in a circle on his cheek. They combed his hair until it was as smooth and fine as the satin hem of a baby's blanket. They unscrewed a lipstick and told him, "Pucker, like you've got yourself a girl to kiss," and my father would pucker in obedience, imagining his mysterious mother—pale, almost transparent, lovely, rarely seen. Then they would apply the lipstick, blot the excess with a tissue. "So pretty," they would say, all three girls standing behind him and looking at his reflection in the mirror.

Even through the rouge they could see that he was blushing, but his trust in them was complete. Never would they shriek, "Fooled you!" and laugh at him, then run screaming and giggling from the room.

The girls had a warm, narcotic effect upon my little boy father, lulling him into a sort of drowsy, perpetual gorged joy. In the sweltering heat of their Georgia home's small, rosebud-papered rooms, they did everything for him. And he, enchanted by these three sweet-smelling, cool-fingered creatures, was devoted to them, utterly.

Granddaddy Dandy was beside himself to have a little man in the house. While he adored his daughters, he did have *four* of them. Yes, he knew that with these girls there would be more trouble ahead. He couldn't keep the boys away with a shotgun forever. Sooner or later, all the rest of them would fall in love and then there would be weddings and tears and more kitchen appliances to buy. He couldn't have known it then, but in just a few years, Dixie the Baby would elope with one of Dandy's own jockeys—*an abomination!*—and they would flee to Havana, hysterical newlyweds on the run. Dandy would take off after them with his Winchester, have the marriage annulled, and threaten the jockey's life if he ever so much as *dreamed* of his baby Dixie again. Dandy could be mean as a snake when he had to be, and with four daughters, he had to be.

So certain was he that these girls would—sooner rather than later—be the end of him, he'd already purchased his plot at the Chickamauga cemetery. Thus, to have a boy, at last! Like a drink of cool water from the deep, deep well.

Hand in hand, they walked every morning to his drugstore on the main street. "Young sir, would you like to do us the honor?" he asked, passing the bronze key to my father. Standing up as straight as he could, maybe even rising up on his toes, my father unlocked the door and followed Dandy into the rear office.

Dandy spent the day standing in his starched white coat behind the pharmacy counter, filling orders to soothe the ailments of the Chickamauga citizens: Dr. Pitcher's Castoria Mint (known as "the pleasant laxative," and always asked for in a furtive whisper), Pinex Throat Medication (both the sheriff and the mailman would testify to its efficacy), and, of course, Azomis Baby Powder for hot, rashy infants, and DeWitt's Golden Liniment for burns, scalds, toothaches, and general lameness. It was rumored that Widow Henderson even used it as a beauty cream beneath her eyes, a peculiar vanity that was generally forgiven due to the unspeakable nature of her tragedy as such a young widow.

Dandy wore gold spectacles and counted pills with supreme accuracy. He impressed upon my father the importance of meticulous counting: "Just one pill of the wrong variety and you could take a life. Always remember that, little buddy."

My father, meanwhile, amused himself behind the soda fountain making root beer floats and banana splits with what ought to have been an illegal amount of chocolate syrup. He thumbed through the comic books, careful not to wrinkle their pages. He sat on the tall stools at the counter and swung his feet back and forth while he softly sang along to the radio, especially "Boogie Woogie Bugle Boy" by the Andrews Sisters, his favorite song, which the station didn't play often enough to suit him.

Tall amber glass bottles stood in a long row on the top shelf behind the soda fountain and sometimes Dandy would send my father up a ladder to retrieve one, warning, "Careful there, boy, don't drop it."

A small brass-bladed General Electric fan helped keep the air moving. My father liked to speak into it to hear his voice distorted. "Hello in there," he'd call, the spin of the blades pitching his voice high and lending it an exhilarating vibrato.

Perhaps most of all, my father loved to ring up sales on the big cash register, engraved as it was with intricate filigree work. He liked to sort the monies into their proper compartments and sometimes the occasional generous (and well-to-do) customer let him keep the extra penny here and there.

At night the family ate together around an oval table made from solid mahogany and shined to such a luster you could see your face reflected in its mirrorlike surface. Fried okra, black-eyed peas, cornbread baked in a cast-iron skillet, ham so salty you had to take a drink of milk after every bite, turnip greens drizzled with vinegar, crispy fried chicken, biscuits that split apart into steaming, paper-thin layers.

When he turned eight, his parents came to collect him. A mother and father he'd known only from pictures swooped down like birds of prey from the darkened sky and hooked him away from Dandy and the aunts.

The reunited family moved first to Athens, then Pensacola, before settling in Tampa. Jack sold Koolvent awnings to people wanting to block out the sun, a bare necessity of life in the deep south.

"You're mine now, boy," his daddy said. On their first night together, my father asked for a bedtime story and Jack whipped his bottom with a leather belt. "They sure as hell spoiled you rotten."

Jack drank every night and he was angry as hell, but over

what nobody could ever figure. My father climbed into his mama's lap for protection, but Carolyn was practically a child herself and every bit as terrified as her son.

When my father spoke of his early childhood, he smiled and remembered every detail, even the tiniest. He wouldn't look at me as he spoke, as though he were remembering privately and I was eavesdropping. But when I asked him what it was like to suddenly live with his parents after all those years of not knowing them, for this is the part that interested me most, my father looked at me, startled, as if I had spontaneously appeared before him like a fist of ball lightning. He became angry and his memory failed him. "Well, it was just very different," is all he'd say. "It wasn't a happy time, that's all. It wasn't a happy time." And then he'd send me away. "I have papers to grade here and I'm tired, very tired."

I turned, began to walk away. My father said, "Son? If you like, you could come with me to the university tomorrow."

Thrilled, as though he'd just told me we were getting a helicopter and a pony, I said, "Really? Okay!" I had trouble going to sleep, images of my father in the drugstore with his grandfather merging with my fantasy of going into school with my father.

But at the university the next day my father sat at his desk doing paperwork. When he saw that I had drawn shapes on his chalkboard he was furious. "Goddamn it, that is not for you to touch. The writing on that board represents a lot of time, do you hear? An awful lot of time." My father had written whole paragraphs on the boards and I avoided those areas, drawing my silly shapes, some of which had arms and feet, only in the unused corners. "But I didn't mess anything up," I whispered.

"This was a bad idea," he fumed. I could see on his face that I had behaved terribly, that drawing on his chalkboard was one of the worst things I'd ever done. His small, angry eyes, creased forehead, and painful frown created a mask of misery and regret. It was exactly the same face I saw on him when he and my mother fought, when the hate was thick between them.

Then he smiled. His dry lips peeled open revealing his foul teeth and his black throat. There was nothing happy in that smile, however. It chilled the room. "You're a lot like your mother," he said.

He did, I realized, think of me as a smaller version of her. I was her *thing,* her creation. Secretly, this pleased me as I took it to mean I wouldn't turn into him when I was grown up. But a wiser, more knowing part of me understood this to be false. That the ways of genetics were fickle and I could, indeed, wake up one day to find my father looking back at me from the mirror. Already, I had his nose and mouth.

I wondered again if maybe I really had another father somewhere. A brief fluttering sensation in my chest signaled excitement and hope. Someday, I would find him.

"Augusten, I have told you again and again, your father is your father," my mother told me. But maybe when I was born a nurse at the hospital made a mistake and gave me to the wrong parents. My mother said the hospital where I was born isn't there anymore. Maybe they mixed up a lot of kids and the police made them close. My mother said the hospital where I was born is a parking lot now. Maybe they gave so many babies to the wrong people that they had to build a new big parking lot to hold all the cars of all the parents who came back to get their correct babies.

In my treasure box was a tiny bracelet a nurse put on my wrist right after I was born. Blue and white beads spelled out my mother's name: M. ROBISON. It was so small I could wear it as a ring.

Oh, it just *had* to be true. Never mind that I had my father's features.

Somewhere in the world was my real father, and he thought about me every day. Maybe he had a chalkboard with colored chalk, not just boring white. Maybe he had a pharmacy, too, and a soda fountain, and pretty aunts in long dresses embroidered with tiny roses you could stroke with your thumb.

I ran from my father's office, turned left, and took off down the long hallway past closed office doors and classrooms, my sneakers squealing on the linoleum tile floor. At the end of the corridor before me, I imagined a man, arms outstretched. I wanted to run into his arms as he hugged me and said the word *Son*.

MY GRANDMOTHER CAROLYN sent me a package of balloons in the mail, the kind that inflate into tubes and you can twist and shape into animals. There were instructions but I wouldn't read them. "Will you?" I asked my father, gently poking him on the elbow. "Will you look at them and show me how to make a dog?"

But my father said, "Not just now, son. I'm very busy."

He was sitting at the kitchen table, staring at the small color television on the counter across from him. The TV was off. That didn't seem very busy to me. So I just stood right there and waited.

On the wall beside him were bookshelves he had installed

himself. I had helped by handing him the screws. That was a long time ago and I almost couldn't remember the day we put the shelves up, except that he'd told me never to climb on them and so that's why I wanted to climb on them. The whole house was new back then. It was clean. It didn't have skin inside, just the bones. It was like a cake in the oven that you couldn't eat yet because it wasn't ready. It had to be ready so you could eat it but it was hot at first so my mother would put it on the stove and say, "Be very careful, don't you touch this pan. It will burn your precious fingers."

If you ate potatoes before they were ready you could get a stomachache. But you *could* eat cake before it was ready because I had licked the spoon.

I had precious fingers.

I had balloons in my fingers.

My father still wouldn't look at me because he was busy.

I wanted to make a balloon dog to go with the real dogs we had. I liked to pet their heads smooth. Their ears would go flat and their eyes would close and they were like seals.

They would eat a macaroni noodle from your lips if you put it there. And they wouldn't touch your lips at all, not even a little. They were very careful and polite, people-dogs.

I tapped my father on the elbow again. "But, if you could show me how to make them? Then I could make them," I said. "And? I would make one for you, too. The best one, you could have it. To keep."

My father did not look away from the television and carefully enunciated his words. "As I told you not three minutes ago, I am very busy and do not have time right now. I would like you to please respect that, son. Now, run along."

My father was sitting at the kitchen table, smoking a

cigarette and drinking his drink and looking at the off TV and I couldn't see how he was busy because there was nothing to be busy *with*.

I missed my mother. She was at the store where you could buy paint brushes and paint in every color that existed in the whole world, even colors between the colors.

"When will my mother be home?" I asked again. I had asked him the same question all afternoon.

"I don't *know*, son. Now *please*," he answered.

I knew that if my mother were there, she would show me how to make a balloon dog and also tell me stories. Unless she was sad and then she wouldn't. But when she wasn't sad, she told me all the stories. Like about her sister who was born with problems and who had arms that were bent and then she died when she was nine. And the undertaker had to break her arms to fit them in the coffin. That was a good story but it was sad because Harriet would have been my aunt and would have sent me presents. And she told me about her big brother who used all his money in the whole world to buy the wedding ring that she gave to my father when they were married. I told my brother and said that he should buy me a ring, too. And he gave me a ring but it was only a trick ring made out of copper wire and it wouldn't even fit on my finger, that's how mean he was. Sometimes, he was too mean to even live.

And she told me there were rattlesnakes in the bamboo patches behind the house where she grew up.

And she told me about aunts and uncles and cousins I didn't even know were all mine. I came from people and there were a lot of them and they lived in Georgia and they were my relations. And my mother and father moved to the north and that was why I liked the snow.

I pressed my lips together and then I asked my father, "What are you busy with?"

And my father slammed his glass down on the kitchen table so hard the table knocked against the wall and liquid splashed out of his glass and landed on my forehead. "Damn it, son. I have told you again and again that I need to be left alone. Now, why is it that you insist on asking me all these questions? I am tired, I don't feel good. I have work to do for school."

I went away. Clutching my small bag of balloons, I padded down the hallway into my room.

My father was busy because he worked at the university. He was a teacher, just like Mr. Nester at school, except my father taught big people, grown-ups.

In my bedroom, I stripped the covers from the bed. I took the blue blanket and placed it over my desk chair. Then I dragged my bedside table across the floor and I placed this near the chair. I draped the remainder of the blanket over this table. Then I crawled inside. I had made a Goonie House.

Best of all was when I made a Goonie House in the living room and my mother got down on her hands and knees and poked her head inside. "I see you," she would say. And I would kiss her nose.

But she wasn't here now and so her head didn't appear at the door of my Goonie House. I sat for a moment and shivered because I felt so cozy. But then I decided to visit my father again, because maybe he was no longer busy.

"Hi," I said, walking back into the kitchen to stand beside him.

He stared straight ahead at the television. The muscles in his jaw tensed and relaxed, tensed and relaxed, as though he were chewing something very small, like a seed.

Because he didn't answer me I said it again.

"*Hi.*"

My father moved so fast that I flinched. He leaped up out of the chair and lunged forward, gripping my shoulders within his massive hands. He squeezed hard, and I winced. His fingers pressed deep into the flesh beneath my shoulder blades and it hurt so much that I suddenly felt warm and nauseous.

He shook me back and forth. "Goddamn you," he spit in my face. "Just this barrage of incessant talking, on and on and on." He stopped shaking me and spun me around so that my left shoulder was pressed into his stomach. With his right hand he spanked me on the bottom, hard. So hard that my pelvic bone would ache for a week and the bruise would spread to my lower back.

"Now, you have to learn that you cannot simply dominate a room and the thoughts and attentions of every person in that room simply because *you* are in it. Goddamn it, Augusten." He continued spanking me until my knees gave out and I folded onto the floor.

At last, he took his seat. "Now, you get up and you go on back to your room and you stay there until your mother gets home. Do you hear me?"

Without looking at him I nodded and tried to stand but I couldn't. So I crawled out of the kitchen on all fours, like a dog. Like a balloon dog. I made it to my room, where I eased into my Goonie House.

He'd spanked my bottom but it was my head that hurt, a hammering sharp pain. I tried to sit, but the pain was worse so I curled up on my side. But that hurt, too. So I lay on my stomach. I closed my eyes and was soon asleep.

My father, seeing the package of balloons on the kitchen floor, picked them up and placed them in the trash can in the kitchen. I would find them there the next day but I would not remove them.

FIVE

ON SATURDAY MORNINGS my parents slept in very late, as though they'd been grave-digging all night. It might be noon, even two or three before I saw them. Awake, alone, I watched TV and ate vanilla cake frosting straight from the can with a spoon. The sugar and the cartoons, speedy and colorful, made me unbearably fidgety. During commercials, I sat on the bare wood floor, raised my knees to my chest, and spun myself around on my tailbone. I gained only enough momentum for a few quick rotations before tipping over on my side, but it was enough to make me dizzy and cause the room to sway and heave, as if it were a ship and not a house on solid ground.

I should have run as fast as I could down the street, all the way to the reservoir and back, exhausted myself, wore myself out. But instead, I stayed indoors, the volume on the TV all the way up, and spun in place. Or, wearing socks, I slid across the kitchen floor into the living room and around the central carpet beneath the dining room table. I slid until my sock bottoms attracted enough dirt and grit that they started to grip instead of slide.

When the cartoons began thinning out, replaced by dreary religious shows and worse, sports, and my sugar high had peaked and I found myself on the other side, spiraling down, tumbling, a sense of emptiness and loneliness overtook me. Sunlight drenched the house, streaming in through a series of wide, sliding glass doors and the large geometric windows above them. But when I peered downstairs the steps merged with darkness and I knew that within that darkness, warm and sleeping, I would find my parents.

Quietly, gently, I padded down the steps. At the bottom, I stood before their closed bedroom door. I pressed my ear to the wood, heard nothing.

I opened the door and entered the cool, dark room. The dehumidifier hummed; it was never turned off, yet the air had a lingering dampness that never went away. My father emptied the two-gallon reservoir daily, but somehow the air remained moist and swampy. I disliked this machine, which seemed to do nothing except pee all day and require constant attention. Secretly, I referred to it as "Harriet," after my mother's brain-damaged baby sister, long dead.

In the dark I crossed the room and found them in their bed, each lying on their side away from the other, creating a wide empty space in the center between them. For me. Suddenly, I was drowsy, so sleepy I could hardly stand on my feet one more instant. Quietly, I entered the bed and crawled over the covers, careful not to bump their sleeping forms.

But my mother stirred, made a sound, not quite a mumble. In her sleep, she was aware of me. Her arm unconsciously lifted the covers beside her, welcoming me in, under.

I crawled beneath the thick soft comforter. My feet, stripped of the filthy socks, were icy against their warm bodies.

I snuggled against my mother, pressed my face into her neck, inhaled her most familiar smell. It was the aroma of my home, where I belonged, everything safe and wonderful.

But I was restless and just as soon as I settled in against her, I turned over onto my other side. I bumped my way over until I was pressed against my father.

He awoke, turned over on his back.

"Augusten, is that you? Oh, now, now, now," he said, raising himself up on his elbows. "Son, no. You can't come down here and mess up our sleep, go on. Go on now." He lifted the covers and pulled them all the way down, exposing me entirely.

I clung to him, wrapping my left arm across his chest.

"Go now, go. You're too old for this, you're not a baby anymore. You have your own bed upstairs in your own room."

When I didn't move, he said angrily, "I mean it, now." He stared at me, his dark eyes furious. "Go. Now."

Stricken, too shocked by this expulsion, I didn't complain. I climbed out of the bed leaving their warmth. I was ashamed. *Too old for this.*

My mother had woken up as well. She looked at me with tenderness and something else, something that broke my heart a little bit. She mouthed the words, *"I'm so sorry."*

Once I was out of the bed, my father lay back down and repositioned the covers beneath his chin. His head was on the pillow but his eyes were open to make sure I actually left.

"And close that door," he said finally.

I closed the door.

• • •

MONTHS LATER, MY father was sitting in the living room in front of the television in his Shaker rocking chair, watching college football and sipping his drink. Dressed in his familiar khaki slacks and gray woolen shirt, his lap was too inviting, so I tried to climb up his legs.

I wanted to curl up there and sleep while he watched the game.

I was still small enough to fit.

But when I tried, he swatted me away. "Get down," he said, eyes on the game. "Get down."

I withdrew. I sat on the floor, mad, and looked at him. I at least wanted him to glance at me so that he could see my mad face and feel bad. I worked hard not to smile, maintaining my mad stare. But the concentration involved made me finally laugh out loud.

Without looking at me, he took a sip of his drink, eyes fixed on the screen.

And this surprised me. I'd done nothing to him, nothing bad and yet he wouldn't even *look* at me. I thought about it some more and realized that he *never* allowed me in his lap. And that was not *fair*.

I was very concerned with what was fair and what wasn't. If my big brother got two scoops of vanilla ice cream, I wanted two scoops. Even if I could only eat the one. My mother said, "But he's a teenager," as if that should justify extra privileges. As far as I was concerned, the only thing teenagers deserved more of was punishment. After all, my big, stupid brother couldn't even aim into the toilet; the rusty radiator beside it was all the proof you needed. Fair is fair and fair is equal.

I was now aware that my father pushed me away but I

wanted to see how *often* he pushed me away. Surely, he couldn't push me away forever. So I decided that I would attempt to snuggle with him and count the *go aways* and the *come heres.* This would make me happy. Because sometimes, I had learned, things *seem* to be one way but *are* another. Like, it *seems* that light is white but *really* it's made up of all the colors. I learned that from my brother who was shocked that I didn't already know it. All a rainbow is is light that walks behind a raindrop and its colors fall out.

I was a willful thing and now I had a plan through which to channel my ambition. For three days, I undertook my experiment, going so far as to actually borrow my mother's clipboard so that I could feel terribly official. It required every fiber of restraint I possessed not to burst out laughing or giggle, *I've got a secret, I'm a scientist!* when my father glanced at me to make sure I wasn't playing with his cigarette lighter. My plan was to confront him with the data and say, "See? It's not fair. I should get to sit up on your lap much more than you let me." I imagined him laughing and scooping me up. "You're absolutely right!"

When I saw him sitting in his rocking chair, or watching television, when he was lying downstairs in his bedroom taking a nap and when he came home from work, I called his name in celebration and attempted to climb into his lap.

I did not need to count the number of checks on the little scorecard I had drawn to see that always, one hundred percent of the time, my father pushed me away. My father would never cuddle with me. I was not allowed in his lap, beside him in bed, or next to him on the sofa with my head on his shoulder. His rebukes were mild but they were consistent. "No, not right now."

I decided this had been a terrible experiment in the first place. I returned the clipboard to my mother's office and then clutched my little scorecard in my hand and carried it to the trash can in the kitchen. I buried it, because the only thing worse than the results of my experiment would be for some-body to see the card and know I had carried it out in the first, pitiful place.

ONE EVENING WHEN my mother was in her office typing and my father was still at the university, I sneaked into their bed-room and rifled through my father's side of the dresser.

I found a pair of slacks I had not seen him wear lately and pulled them from the drawer. In the bathroom closet I pawed through the various shirts, jackets, and dresses on hangers until I found a plaid shirt that he would not miss.

He had a drawer of belts, coiled like sleeping snakes. I took one and carried the clothing upstairs to my room and laid it all out on the bed: slacks, shirt, belt through the loops.

I pulled my own top sheet from the tangled mound of blan-kets and worn clothes on the floor at the foot of my bed and be-gan stuffing the corner deep into the leg of the pants. There was enough sheet for both legs but not enough to plump up the shirt, too.

I scurried down the hall and into the bathroom where I swiped the two towels hanging from the shower curtain rod. In the hall, on the way back to my room, I looked over my shoul-der to make sure I wasn't spotted.

Next, I stuffed the shirt, pulling as much towel into each arm as possible, then I tucked the shirt into the slacks.

A headless, footless, modestly stuffed *body* lay on top of my

bed. Outside my window, the crickets maintained their relentless throbbing and the clatter of my mother's typing seemed
to merge with their sound until there was almost a rhythmic
chanting urging me forward: *go, go, go, go, go.* The air in my bedroom had altered, brightened, become charged—like another
person was now in here with me. As I looked at what I'd done,
I felt a pulsing excitement. As well, I felt as if I had solved
something. I'd never been good at math, except the single time
my brother sat down with me and helped me think through a
word problem. When I arrived at the answer on my own, I was
both startled and euphoric. That's how I felt, standing in my
bedroom and looking at what I'd created with my father's un-
worn clothing: a swell of pleasure at having arrived at the answer myself.

Tenderly, being mindful not to dislodge the torso from the
legs and spoil the illusion, I crawled into bed beside the body,
turned on my side, and curled against it.

A trace, a mere whiff of my father's cologne clung to the
shirt's fibers when I pressed my face against its chest. It was an
acceptable substitute.

Drowsiness overtook me like a drug. The father body had an
intoxicating effect on me, and if I had spoken, my words would
have been slurred.

Somehow, I understood that I must not fall asleep. That to be
caught with my stuffed father would get me into a different kind
of trouble. The punishment would have to be as unusual as the
crime and this realization rejuvenated me, pulling me from the
strange, thick sleepiness.

I climbed off the bed and severed the torso from the legs,
stacked them together, folded them once. They would be easy to
reassemble, and in the meantime they appeared to be just a pile

of clothes on the floor of my closet. I pressed the surrounding closet contents—books, stuffed animals, shoes—around it.

Never again would I attempt to snuggle up with my father. Now when I needed him, I would go to my room and assemble the body, place it on the bed, and hug it.

In time, the sheets and towels were replaced with pillows, "guest pillows" for guests that never came.

Periodically, I rubbed a little pine-tar lotion into the shirtsleeve or sprinkled the slacks with Old Spice. I smeared just a little Eucerin cream into the collar. These were my father's scents. And with my head on the stuffed chest of the substitute, I would experience the same sudden, bleary tiredness that had overtaken me the first time. I would sleep, sometimes for ten minutes, sometimes for an hour. And then I would startle awake, flushed with shame, and quickly disassemble it, stowing it hastily in the closet and promising myself that this was the *last* time.

For it had begun to feel somehow wrong, even dangerous. Dangerous to me, and dangerous to other people, though the recognition was dim and I had no idea exactly why. It terrified me to consider: What if, as a grown-up, I craved another body beside me as still as this one? What then?

But at seven, then eight, I was still sleeping with my stuffed father regularly. While not every night, I found I was sleepless without him at least three times a week.

When I considered how much comfort this arrangement gave me, I was sickened. So I refused to think of it. And my stolen, puzzling naps assumed a reckless quality. I was a slave to my need.

When at last my stuffed father was deconstructed it was not by my own hands. My mother discovered the clothes stuffed with pillows in my room. She thought nothing of it, or not enough to mention it. She simply returned the clothes to the closet and placed the extra pillows on my bed. Over time, my father's scents faded from the pillows until there was nothing left of him at all.

SIX

MY FATHER AND I were walking along Market Hill Road in Shutesbury just two houses past our own. My father's black oxford shoes crunched over the loose gravel on the dirt road while I kicked stones and tried to follow their trajectory. "What's the straightest thing?" I asked. I tried to imagine what it could be. A ruler? The sharp edge of a piece of paper?

"What do you mean, son, the straightest thing?"

"I mean, what's the straightest thing in the whole world?"

My father exhaled, weary. "Aw, well, let's see, what would that be?" he asked himself. And as we walked, my father tilted his head to the sky, which was blocked by the pine trees that lined the road. I continued to kick rocks with the rubber toe of my sneaker, shooting pebbles into the ditch that ran alongside us. "Well," he finally said, "I would have to guess that the straightest thing would be a ray of light."

A ray of light.

His answer excited and confused me, propelled me forward so that I was steps ahead of him and had to walk backward to face him. The questions spilled out of me. "But how? How can light be straight? Isn't light just like water and it washes over everything? Light isn't straight. Light isn't a *thing.*"

"Well, rays of light, yes. Those would be the straightest things, I'm pretty sure. It's only an illusion that light is, like you say, water, washing over everything."

Suddenly, I desperately wanted to look at the sun, I wanted to see in the sky a sun radiating pure, straight yellow lines. Like the drawing on a box of Raisin Bran. But the sun was blocked by the trees, these woods were so thick. Our whole neighborhood was just a street carved out of the wilderness, a few houses dropped down into small clearings. How could the rays of the sun be the straightest thing, straighter than a ruler or a piece of paper? "You mean, if you squint?" I asked, narrowing my eyes, instantly seeing rays of light—indeed—streaming through the dense pines. Yes, they were straight, these lines. But how could they be the straightest things? How could you measure?

"Son, I'm tired now. We'd best be heading back home."

We'd only walked the length of four houses. We weren't even past the Abramses' yet, not four hundred feet from our driveway.

My father's limp became pronounced, as though his right leg were sinking into the road with each step. His mouth was a fixed grimace, the lines on his forehead were bowed, as though bearing weight. I knew there would be no argument, no *Just five more minutes.* We would turn around now and walk home.

But this had been something, our first walk together. I didn't know then that it would also be our last. That the memory of this day would remain with me always: the single time my father and I took a walk and spoke of light.

Looking at my father's face, seeing that half of it was in shadow, the other half nearly glowing, I felt engorged with hope.

I was his son and light was the straightest thing in the world and I felt amazed, like when my teacher played a record for us, a mournful, weeping song, and told us it wasn't any instrument at all but the sound of a whale.

"No."

I hadn't asked him a question, I hadn't said a thing.

"No, I just don't feel good, not at all," my father said.

ON MY NINTH birthday my father gave me a baseball glove. It was a beautiful mitt; a Wilson A2100 the color of cooked sugar. Not only had I never had a glove before, I'd never learned to throw a ball and didn't know the rules of the game. For years, I'd sat and observed my father watching baseball games, cutting in now and then and asking, "How does it work? What are the rules?"

"It's difficult to explain," he said. "Just watch the game and see if you can follow along." So I sat back, my gaze alternating between the small television and my father's face, trying to decipher the rules of the game.

Now, I turned the glove over in my hand, slipped my fingers inside.

"Be careful with it," my father said. "You have to break it in. You have to take good care of it. And especially, don't get it wet."

It seemed every moment in my life had led to this one, the

first time my father had taken me aside and given me something special. I held the glove in my hand reverentially. "I will," I said. "I will be *so* careful."

He smiled tightly, slapped me on the back. "Good boy. I'm glad you like your gift."

"Can we go outside?" I asked, embarrassed because I knew I was leaking hope the way our dog Cream would sometimes squirt pee on the floor when she was excited.

He folded himself into the rocking chair in the living room, exhaling loudly as he sat. "Oh, not now. You go play, I'm in a lot of pain."

"Just for a minute?" I begged.

He closed his eyes. "I'm very tired right now. You go on and play with your new glove."

I walked away, carrying the mitt by the wrist strap. The trouble was, I didn't know *how* to play with it.

I knew I should be very grateful for this extraordinary present, but I couldn't help feeling almost sad. Because before I had a glove, I didn't need a father to throw a ball at me.

A ball. That's when it occurred to me, he'd given me a glove but nothing to catch.

THE BASEBALL GLOVE sat alone on the highest bookshelf in my bedroom, a location of honor, high above the record album sleeves, dirty laundry, general clutter. It sat there for months. But it seemed to taunt me from that height, with its wrinkle-free hide, its pristine condition.

One afternoon after school, my mother surprised me with a baseball. "Look what I bought at the store today. Would you like to go out to the backyard and play catch?"

"No," I said. "That's okay. I don't need to."

She smiled at me, bit her bottom lip. "Oh, come on. It'll be fun." With her big toe, the nail painted bright red, she scratched her calf, then hopped to regain her balance. She was in an un- usually perky mood; she'd even set her hair in curlers and then brushed it out. But I knew that one of her good moods was al- ways followed by a very bad one. I figured I better not be the reason.

"Well, all right," I finally agreed. "Let me just go get my glove." And I ran back to my room. I dragged my desk chair over to the bookshelf, stood on the seat, and grabbed the glove.

I followed my mother outside, around the house to the back. She lit a cigarette from the pack she always kept in the front patch pocket of her dress and said, "Okay, you go stand over there at the edge of the woods," and pointed to the very rear boundary of the yard.

I jogged back there, swatting bugs away from my head. I turned around to face her. "Okay," I shouted. The glove felt funny on my hand, heavy.

She brought her cigarette to her lips. "Are you ready?"

"Yeah," I called back, waiting.

She tossed the ball to me, underhand. Even though I ran, I missed it because it only landed a few feet in front of her.

"Sorry," she called. "I'll throw it better the next time." My mother had become expert at speaking around the cigarette in her mouth, squinting her eyes against the smoke.

I handed her the ball and then ran back to my spot at the edge of the yard. I slammed my fist into the glove, because I'd seen players do this, and shouted, "Okay, I'm ready again."

My mother threw the ball again and this time it landed off to the side and rolled into the woods.

It was no use. She didn't know how to play baseball any more than I did. My mother could open a book of matches and remove one and light it using only her toes, but she could not throw a ball.

I picked it up off the ground, wiped away a damp leaf, and then walked back to her. "I don't want to play catch," I said. "We don't have to, it's okay."

"I'm not very good, am I?" she asked, gently tucking a curl out of my face. "Well, maybe your dad can come out after work and play with you for a while."

"He won't do that," I said, and the anger in my voice surprised me. In a more casual voice I added, "He never wants to do anything with me."

I wanted my mother to hug me and say, *That's just not true,* but instead she said, "Well, *I* want to do things with you."

She headed back indoors and I left the glove outside on a rock so that the rain could weather it. I wanted it to at least look like the other boys' gloves, soft and well used. I certainly couldn't bring such a pristine glove to school; I might as well show up in a dress. So I left it on a rock and after a week, dye had leached onto the stone beneath it.

The glove had dried stiff. I'd ruined it.

My mother felt sorry for me. She drove me to the Mountain Farms Mall, where we parked in front of JCPenney. As always, I couldn't resist staring at the tooth imprints on the dashboard of our drab Dodge Aspen wagon. When my parents had brought the Aspen home for the first time, I'd sat in the passenger seat, admiring the new car. Then, because I could not stop myself, I leaned forward and bit into the soft dashboard. The material flexed beneath my bite and when I pulled away, I saw my tooth marks had remained in the dash. Even at the time I'd wondered what had compelled me to bite the dashboard like that. But now, a year older, I groaned inwardly whenever I saw the bite, which was every time I got in the car. It was like a tattoo of my immaturity. Plus, my father had been furious when he saw the damage, screaming, "Jesus Christ, son, what possessed you? Why would you do such a thing?" He couldn't think of a punishment appropriate to the crime, so there had been none. My own mortification had been enough.

"Ready?" my mother said. We climbed out of the car and walked into the mall.

The pet store was, of course, my favorite. Although I visited it each time we went to the mall, I'd only once been allowed to bring something back from it: hermit crabs. The crabs had been fascinating pets, as I invented a rich inner life for them, naming them Gladys, Marshall, Stuart, Gabrielle, and Charlotte. Despite my best efforts, they all died, leaving me with their shells, which my mother, to my horror, wanted to mix with the bowl of decorative seashells in her office. "When Cream dies, will you hang her hide on your wall?" I asked.

We were here today for a guinea pig. My parents wouldn't let me get another dog, but at least my mother understood that another set of crabs just wouldn't cut it. I needed something warm and fuzzy that I could name and snuggle with.

The pet store had an entire wall of small, furry mammals: mice, rats, guinea pigs, hamsters, gerbils. While I liked hamsters, too, the Habitrail cage was expensive. Even I could see that the interconnecting boxes, tubes, and spheres could easily bankrupt a family and lead to addiction later in life. Because, how would you know when to stop? How *could* you stop? An entire city could be built with a Habitrail. My mother understood this at once because when I asked she replied, "No way."

But a guinea pig and an aquarium were modest, so she agreed.

There were so many and they were all cute, and I realized this wouldn't be just a matter of waltzing into the store and pointing to one. I would have to meet each of the pigs and choose one based on its personality, spirit, and innate good manners. Luckily, the clerk was patient and allowed me to cradle every pig I pointed to. I knew I didn't want a long-haired model, those were for girls who liked to comb hair and add repulsive little bows. So I narrowed my search to the short-haired variety.

Still, it was tough. The black ones were sleek and beautiful, but did they look a little like rats, all one color like that?

I could get a white one, but then, why not just get a bunny? "Could I?" I asked my mother.

"Absolutely not. You may select a guinea pig and that's it."

I settled on a tricolor, a little of each. He was tan and white with just a smattering of black. When I pressed him to my chest and he wriggled up against my neck and nuzzled my ear, I named him, Ernest. Ernie for short.

We set up Ernie in his aquarium in the kitchen. The aquarium had a stand, so the top of the tank was well over my head. I had to call my mother or my father to take him out when I wanted to pet him.

Soon, Ernie possessed an impressive repertoire of tricks. He squealed every time the refrigerator was opened and would stop only if some lettuce was deposited on the cedar-shaving-covered floor of his cage. He emitted a different squeal when he wanted to run around on the floor. If I called, "Here, Ernie!" he would run to the side of his aquarium closest to the door, stand up on his little back feet, and wait to be picked up. "Look at you," I said to him, "just a little animal, plucked from nature."

Ernie was so adorable, even my mother, who at first called him "a loaf of rat," came to love him. "He is awfully sweet, isn't he?" she admitted as Ernie crawled across her bosom to nibble on her blue Indian corn necklace.

My mother took many photographs of me and Ernie together—Ernie in one of the costumes I created for him out of fabric scraps and glue, Ernie sitting in a chair just like a person. Though when I strung one of my mother's gigantic bras across the back of two kitchen chairs and set Ernie into one of the cups, like a hammock, she didn't take a picture as I expected but screamed, "Take that horrible thing out of my good bra!" I was insulted that she called Ernie a "horrible thing" and I back-talked her. "He's cuter than what's usually in that big old bra."

Only my brother was uninterested in Ernie. But my brother, I'd come to understand, wasn't interested in living things. Not only would he refuse to make eye contact, my brother wouldn't respond if you spoke to him. You had to walk up to him and scream at the side of his head to get his attention, or jab him really hard with something sharp. That worked.

One morning, an expression of contempt settled on his face when I told him there was no more cereal because I'd fed the last of it to Ernie. He was now in active competition with the little guinea pig for food.

That afternoon I said, "Mom? I'm afraid my brother is going to do something bad to Ernie."

She stopped typing and looked up at me. "What do you mean by bad?" she asked. "Why would you think such a thing?"

I told her, "I just . . . my brother doesn't understand little pets. They aren't cute to him. What if he fed Ernie a battery? What if he cooked him?" Ernie was, after all, in the kitchen, along with all the other ingredients.

My mother continued to look into my eyes, then she reached for her pack of cigarettes and lit one. She inhaled, closing her eyes. *"Okay,"* she said, exhaling in relief. She chewed her thumb nail as she thought about this. Maybe she was remembering the time my brother buried me outside, headfirst. Or perhaps she was recalling when my brother hooked her up to a series of strobe lights when she was sleeping, so that she awakened with a heart-seizing shock to a flashing, confusing light show inches from her face. Even though nobody ever spoke of it, we knew there was just something *different,* perhaps even defective, about my brother. You could see it in photographs of him when he was small, something about his eyes. He had the oddly impersonal gaze of a mischievous farm animal, a goat maybe, but not a boy.

My mother moved Ernie's cage into my bedroom, where he would be safe.

"IT'S OKAY, ERNIE, it's okay boy. Don't worry. This just happens sometimes is all. They'll stop soon, I promise." I was whispering these words into Ernie's ear as I lay in bed with him tucked into the crook of my arm, covers pulled up over us.

My parents were shouting at each other in the living room.

I'd never known life without the sound of my parents' fighting. The shrill, furious screams of my mother, the drunk, bitter reprimands of my father. Though they'd been fighting since I could remember, over the last few years it had escalated. Now I was afraid something might *happen.*

I scratched behind Ernie's little head and he made the softest sound, air rubbing against air, as his whiskers twitched and brushed against the blanket. "Don't worry," I said softly, "we'll be okay."

But I wasn't sure about this, not at all. Sometimes, I'd be able to make out a word: "kill" or "hate" or "die." I didn't want to hear what they were saying, I didn't want to understand one thing. I just wanted them to stop.

As though I had willed it to happen, the house was suddenly silent. I gently ran my index finger down Ernie's nose. "See? It's over, it's all better now."

I silently peeled back the blanket, as though by making even one small sound I would reactivate the battle in the living room, and climbed from the bed, Ernie still cradled in my arms. Gently, I stepped onto the chair I'd placed beside his aquarium and lowered him onto a bed of soft, fragrant cedar chips. I saw that his water bottle was full, but I knew by now it wasn't cold any longer. Normally, I'd run into the bathroom and let the water run until it was icy. Our water came from our own deep well and all other water tasted wrong to me. But that would have to wait. I couldn't risk leaving the security of my room. One thing I could do, though, was scoop out the few soiled chips that I saw, throw them into the trash can, then add a fresh handful.

Ernie circled like a miniature dog then snuggled into a ball. I gently lowered my hand into the aquarium and traced the ir- resistible curve of his precious back. With my finger just barely touching him, I could feel the tiny rise and fall of his body with each breath. Ernie was a happy guinea pig, unlike the one at school that was a small monster, driven mad by the shrieking children, the constant poking and squeezing. The school pig struggled against affection, would nip your finger if you reached for him. Pauline Milkmoore had to see the nurse after it bit her pinkie and drew blood, and I could only hope she would die from rabies. Pauline Milkmoore would run around chasing everybody and shouting, "Smell my finger" after having inserted it into one of her many holes.

My mother opened my door with such force, a gust of wind passed through my room and the curtains swayed. "We're leaving," she said directly. "Pack your bag with underpants, clean socks, a pair of jeans, a sweater, two or three shirts. I need you to hurry, Augusten. Do this right now. You'll need your toothbrush." She turned to leave but I called out, "Wait!" and she froze.

"What is it?" she said, her eyes burning with intensity.

She frightened me. I didn't understand what was happening. Where were we going? But I only said, "What about Ernie?"

I watched her eyes slide to his aquarium, then back at me. "It's okay," she said. "Leave him right where he is. Your father will take care of him. He's staying."

She started to leave but before she could I rushed in with another question: "But where are we going? Why?"

I thought back to the Amherst apartment, Mexico. I didn't want to go. It was like she was asking me to come with her back in time.

"We're just going to a motel, that's all. Just for a couple of nights. Now hurry up and pack." She turned and left.

I did as she said, retrieving my small suitcase from the closet. I opened it on my bed and put in a pair of jeans, a few shirts, socks, underwear. I glanced around my room wondering what else I should take but then I heard the car start up outside my window. I closed the case. "Okay, Ernie, be good," I said. But he was sleeping. And I wouldn't dare wake him up for this.

Carrying my suitcase, I stepped as softly as I could down the hallway to the front door. I didn't see my father or my brother. The front door was open, so I just stepped outside and closed it

behind me. My mother was in the car, the dome light illuminat-
ing her drawn, gaunt face. She looked frightened and this made
me worried. Something was wrong.

I placed my suitcase in the back, then climbed into the car,
feeling like I was in some sort of fever dream, where things
aren't quite right somehow; colors too bright, sounds unnatural,
the scale of things all messed up. "What happened?" I asked
after I settled myself in the seat.

She put the car in reverse, looking wild-eyed over her right
shoulder as she backed down the driveway. She shifted into
drive and we set off.

"Your father and I had a fight and I don't want us sleeping at
the house tonight. He's very drunk and I don't think it's safe."

Something heavy shifted out of position within my chest.
There was that word again, *safe*. We hadn't been safe before and
we'd had to live in an apartment. "Are we going back to
Amherst?" I couldn't help asking, and my voice sounded younger
to my ears, and I felt younger, too. Things were terribly wrong
and I wasn't one hundred percent sure I *wasn't* actually dreaming, sick and high-fevered, shaking in bed.

"No," she said, "we're just going away for a night or two.
Three at the most. Just until your father settles down and we can
work this out. Don't you worry," she said, looking over at me.

"What about my brother?" I asked, wondering why he
wasn't coming with us, too.

"Your brother's fine, don't worry," she said. "He's staying at
home with your father."

Why was *he* safe and we weren't?

The question remained unasked and unanswered. My mother
crushed her cigarette into the ashtray, which was overflowing
with butts, and immediately lit another.

• • •

WE CHECKED INTO a Holiday Inn just off Interstate 91 in Northampton. The first thing I did was stand on the bed and touch the rough, sparkly ceiling. I could just reach it. As I drew my finger across the coarse, prickly surface I enjoyed a sense of relief and fulfillment—it felt exactly as I knew it would. Sometimes, I would be sitting next to my mother in the car looking out the window when I saw a fence or a stone wall. "Pull over, please," I would cry and my mother would slide the car over to the shoulder. I'd been watching the fence or the stone wall and imagining running my fingers across it, could almost experience what it would feel like to the touch. And I simply had to see if I was right, if it felt the way I thought it would feel. It was like this with the ceiling.

My mother grabbed the telephone and carried it over to the bed. She made a pile of pillows behind her back, lit a cigarette, and settled in.

I turned on the television and my mother automatically made a motion with her hand, lower the volume.

She called her friend Gayle and spoke in a weary, fatigued whisper. "I took Augusten and left the house." She pulled on her cigarette and blew the smoke above the mouthpiece of the phone. "Yes, exactly," she said. "That's what I was worried about. So we're fine now. We're here and I'll phone the doctor in the morning. Hopefully he can work on John."

It was hard to focus on the television and not eavesdrop on what my mother was saying. I began worrying about Ernie. Would my father just give him his regular food, or would he remember to give him treats? He had been the one who'd first given Ernie some carrots, so I wasn't too worried.

My mother didn't stay on the phone for long. She hung up and told me, "I have some dimes if you want to run down to the vending machine for a snack."

The vivid paisley print of my mother's hand-sewn cotton dress nearly throbbed in the drab room, which was lit only by a single lamp, its shade yellowed and stained. Now, being alone with her again, on the run, unsafe, I felt as though everything I knew was folding in on itself. My stomach faithfully cramped. "I wish we'd brought a hot water bottle," I mumbled.

"Oh, is your stomach bothering you again?" she said, and just the way she said it soothed me.

"Yes," I answered.

She pulled me close and placed her warm hand on my stomach. "Shhhh," she said, gently kissing my forehead. "It's okay." And even though I knew that it wasn't, I let it be.

She smelled like metal.

I wanted to sleep.

We slept.

In the morning, my mother called my school and told them I would be out for a few days.

We breakfasted on eggs over easy and dry white toast at a diner. The parking lot was filled with tractor trailers.

My mother smoked and pushed her plate away untouched.

"Did you sleep, Mom?"

"A little."

"You look so tired. Are you okay?" Her cheeks appeared hollow and gaunt, and her eyes, bloodshot, had a haunted look that I didn't like at all.

Almost under her breath she said, "Finish your eggs, at least the white part."

I looked at the sprig of parsley on my plate and wondered if

Ernie would eat it. I wanted to fold it into a napkin and bring it home for him. But when would we be home again?

By the evening of the second night my mother had seen her psychiatrist and spoken to my father on the phone. I'd remained close to her side, except at the doctor's office, where I waited for her in the reception room.

"We'll go home tomorrow," she told me.

"Can we go tonight?"

"No. Tomorrow."

Finally I asked her, "What happened?"

She looked thoughtfully at me and then seemed to decide something. "Your father has been drinking very heavily lately, and the other night when we were having that fight he wrapped his hands around my neck. I managed to kick him in the knee and free myself."

I just watched her.

"So I didn't think we should stay in the house anymore. I was worried that he was dangerous. Your father needed some time to settle down," she told me.

I held the word in my mouth before letting it out. "Danger-ous." What was this unspeakable danger, which had the quality of a dream evaporating just after waking? A name, but no shape. What was it about him that made me wary even when he wasn't drunk? And whatever it was, did I have it within me, too?

She stared into my eyes and her face held an expression as articulate as the words: *you know.*

I could always read my mother by looking at her eyes. Whether she was happy or sad or frightened or upset, it was just right there. I thought of my father's eyes. And how they revealed absolutely nothing. When I looked at him, I saw only my own questioning, searching gaze reflected back at me.

• • •

WE DID NOT go home the next day. Or the day after that. We stayed away from home for seven more days.

My mother saw her psychiatrist each afternoon, sometimes joined by my father. I was watched by Mr. Rice who managed the motel or simply locked in the room and told not to open the door for anyone. I remained out of school, growing so far behind I would be forced to repeat the third grade the following year.

I longed for Ernie and begged my mother to let us get him. "We can't, Augusten. He has that huge aquarium and besides, we can't have pets at the motel. Your father is watching him. Your father said Ernie's very happy and he's getting plenty of attention."

"You asked him?"

"Yes, I did. And he said Ernie is fine."

"But I want to go home."

"I know. And we will, soon."

The days lost their definition for me; morning and evening were identical because I spent both staring at the television. I took naps and then had trouble sleeping at night. I woke up confused, unsure of where I was. I almost never left the room and if I did it was only to walk along the concrete landing to the vending machines where I would buy a Coke or peanut M&M's. The days seemed to double in length and there was nothing to do but wait. I felt suspended, like when the swing reaches the top bar and pauses in midair, or when you think you're going to sneeze but don't.

And then finally, my mother told me to pack. "We're going home." And as suddenly as we'd left the red house, we returned to it.

When we pulled into the driveway, I started to bounce in my seat. The weight of all the previous days evaporated and I was just happy to be home. I opened the door before my mother had come to a stop.

"Don't," she shouted. "Wait until I've parked."

The moment she stopped, I leaped out of the car. I bounded up the front steps and opened the front door. My father was standing in the doorway of the kitchen, a smile on his face. "Well, hello there," he said. His voice was low and steady, but there was something curious in his tone.

"Hi," I said, not sure if I should go to him and try and hug him or just walk past him to my room.

"Did you have a fun trip?" he asked.

I stood ten feet in front of him and replied nervously, "I guess."

My mother appeared behind me, closing the door. She walked past me, faced my father. He turned sideways in the doorway, allowing her to pass. She strode past him, went to the cabinet, and retrieved a glass. She filled it with water from the faucet and drank thirstily, the knob of her throat rising and falling.

I turned, then ran down the hallway, opened the door to my room. "Ernie, Ernie, Ernie," I called in the playful, nasal voice I often used with him. "ErnieErnieErnie." His name, spoken in this way, created a noise that sounded very much like the sound he emitted when the refrigerator door was opened or he saw me enter the room with a carrot.

My room was dark, the curtains pulled tight. I turned on the light.

The glass walls of the aquarium were glazed with filth; crusty brown feces, rotten, liquefied lettuce. Claw marks were etched onto the glass walls, all over in a frantic, crazy pattern. The floor of the aquarium was filled with an inch of festering black fluid; rancid cedar chips and feces floated on top. His water bottle and food bowl were empty.

Ernie, his hair matted, crispy, lay rigid in the sludge, his feces-caked mouth open in a scream. His eyes were white and cloudy.

I started to shake. I couldn't control myself. Even my legs were trembling and my teeth began to chatter, like I was freezing cold. I let go of my suitcase handle and it fell onto the floor. The thud made me flinch. I ran from my room.

My father watched me walking toward him. His arms down at his sides, he smiled, his eyes unreadable. "Did you say hello to Ernie?"

Still trembling, I stared at his mouth, his crooked, stained teeth, rotten in front. When I finally spoke my voice was broken, rough. "Where is my mother?"

"She's gone out to visit her friend, Gayle."

My father turned away from me and walked into the kitchen. He poured himself a glass of iced tea from the brown plastic pitcher that always sat next to the dish drainer. He carried his drink downstairs to the basement.

AND IT BEGAN.

Hate unspooled within my chest. *Hate* bloomed within me, unfurling like the supple petals of a deadly flower—oleander, foxglove.

My childhood was over now. A part of me had died. But another part was born.

And I knew that whatever badness my father had within

him, I had within me, too. Before, I was afraid that I might grow up to be like him. Now, I knew that I already was. Because what he had done to Ernie I knew I could do to him.

My father did not deserve to breathe.

SEVEN

A<small>S LATE AFTERNOON</small> light filled the room with melancholy pink and gold, and long shadows reached across the floor pulling darkness into the room, my mother stood at her old easel, its fine wood grain humbled by gouges and splotches of long-dried paint. The easel stood in front of the sliding glass doors in the living room. She wore another dress she'd made herself: red cotton with a scoop neck. She was barefoot and wore no jewelry but for her wide gold wedding band. In her left hand she balanced her wooden palate, stained with thick, glossy oil paint—cobalt blue, cadmium yellow, purple madder, quinacridone magenta, raw umber, and sap green. A years-old Maxwell House coffee can filled with brushes and a turpentine-soaked rag rested on the old red chair she'd dragged up from the basement. The chair had belonged to my father's grandmother, Dandy's wife "Mamaw," a name that to me always eerily evoked a praying mantis in a black dress and hat. The chair had once been part of a set around her kitchen table but the others were long gone. My mother had painted it first blue then red, and briefly it had been in my bedroom, where I had discovered just how uncomfortable it was. Now it held paint supplies.

"Honey, guinea pigs don't live for years and years like dogs. They die. It's very sad, but they don't live a long time. Ernie had a very good life, he was a happy little animal."

I stood beside her, begging for attention, anxiously clenching my fingers into fists. "But Ernie didn't die naturally. My father killed him. He starved him and didn't give him water. You saw his cage. Why did he do that?"

"Your father didn't kill Ernie, Augusten. He took care of him, fed him, and gave him water. Ernie was probably sick and we didn't know it."

"Mom," I cried in frustration, stamping my feet, desperate for her to understand, "Ernie was *not* sick, I would have known. His cage couldn't have become so"—and I pictured the cage, the unspeakable filth—"*dirty* in just a day!"

"Look, your father was very upset when he found out Ernie was dead. He said he had no idea, he'd checked on him just that morning and Ernie was walking around in his cage making noises."

It was a lie. My father *had* killed Ernie and my mother was too preoccupied to see this.

On her canvas a face was beginning to emerge, the features outlined softly in pencil. Paint had been applied only to the background, the ruffled collar and shoulder of the dress. An old black-and-white photograph of her grandmother was attached to the upper left corner of the canvas with a piece of masking tape.

My father was downstairs in my parents' bedroom, watching

television. Earlier, he'd carried the heavy aquarium into the woods, dumped its contents, then carried it back into the front yard, where he'd hosed it out. The clean aquarium was now downstairs in the basement.

I would never step near it again.

My brother, as usual, was barricaded in his bedroom, the scent of his soldering iron filling that end of the house as he welded tiny electronic components together to create something no one could understand.

Everybody was behaving as though nothing was shockingly wrong and it was making me crazy.

"Augusten, I'm sorry your pet died, but death is a part of life. Now, let me get back to my painting. If you want to stand here with me and watch, that's fine." She smudged the line of the jaw with her finger, then stood back from the canvas, squinting and cocking her head. "Did I ever tell you how I met your father?" she asked, not taking her eyes off her canvas.

Ernie didn't die naturally and I knew it. *I knew it, I knew it, I knew it.*

"Hmmmm?" she said, glancing over at me.

"Yes," I said distractedly. She'd told me the story of how she met my father so many times it felt like my own. Much of her repeated lore had taken on that quality.

I only wanted her to understand what had happened, what my father had done. If she would only sit down and focus, if she would only listen.

But then, I decided I *did* want to hear the story. I wanted to curl up and close my eyes and just listen to her talk and talk and talk.

"Okay," I said in a small voice, "tell me again."

She leaned into her canvas and, with her brush loaded with

the palest blue, began to paint a pearl button onto the high collar below the subject's chin. "Well, we were both freshmen at
the University of Georgia. This would have been in 1952. Our
first class was English and the class was seated alphabetically,
according to our last names. My last name was Richter and your
father's was Robison, so we sat right next to each other. I
looked to my right and there was your father. Of course, I didn't
know this when I looked at him."

She glanced down at me and smiled, a brush in her right
hand like a wand, as though she'd just used it to conjure me.

This was the part of the story where I always felt the most
amazement. What if somebody at the university had spelled
their names wrong on the sheet? Or left out a letter? Would I
still have been born, though perhaps missing an ear?

"Your father said hello to me. And after class, we walked together and talked. We started dating. Your father had very good
manners. He had ambitions of becoming a minister."

I stared at her hands. The way she could make just a tiny
splotch of paint look like a pearl that you could reach out and
touch. With her finest brush tapered to a hair-thin point she
added a small window of white to the blue and gray of the pearl,
creating a perfect reflection.

"Well, Mother loved your father. And Daddy liked him,
too. They felt he was a very respectable young man and he
was."

She dipped the brush in turpentine and wiped it with her
rag. She took a step back and continued. "Of course, your father
was on the track team back then. And he was a high-jumper. I
remember, he could jump over six feet. Maybe it was six feet
and two inches. I remember him telling me that he was very
close to the figure that won the 1948 Olympics, which I seem to

remember his telling me was about six and a half feet. So your father was a real athlete."

It was impossible to imagine my father running and jumping. Now, he was an athlete only in the misery Olympics. My father, who clutched his knee in pain after climbing the stairs, who grit his teeth just because he was standing up from the kitchen table. And then because my heart had started to race, I stopped thinking of my father. I watched my mother's lips as she spoke, instead.

"Well, finally after a few months your father proposed. I remember we were walking and he seemed so nervous. At one point he just stopped right there on the path and his hands were shaking. He turned to me and out of the blue asked me if I would marry him.

"But at this point, you see I didn't want to be married, not to anyone. I wanted to be a painter and live in Paris or Greenwich Village in New York City.

"But your father told me that if I didn't marry him, that he would kill himself."

My mother reached into the patch pocket on her dress and brought out her cigarettes. She lit one and stared at her painting, blowing smoke. "Mother wanted me to marry him. Mother told me, 'This is what you do, Margaret. He's a good man and he's asked you and you must say yes.' I remember your father's eyes, so dark, and I was terrified. I was sure that if I turned him down he really would shoot himself in the face so I said yes. It wasn't long after that we were married at Mother's house down in Cairo. Just a small wedding." Her voice had dropped to nearly a whisper.

"What was it like?" I asked.

As she spoke, she gazed into the air above my head, absently twisting the wedding band on her left hand with the thumb and forefinger of her right. Around and around she turned it, as though unscrewing the lid to her past.

Most of the living room furniture had been moved out of the room, but footprints from the sofa, coffee table, and chairs remained indented in the floral carpeting. A white fabric runner had been unrolled atop the carpet, extending from the fireplace across the room, to the position where the minister would stand. My mother's white satin heels constantly caught on the runner.

Hours before the guests arrived, my mother's mother had placed a bouquet of white flowers on top of the mantel. White carnations, lilies, and ferns. She placed a similar arrangement on the buffet, between two tall silver candlesticks.

My father's parents had dressed in a surprisingly somber fashion for a wedding. With my grandfather's charcoal suit and black tie and my grandmother's deep red dress, belted so tightly at the waist a deep breath would have been impossible, they looked like guests at a funeral and not a wedding.

But nobody could have mistaken my mother for anything other than a bride. At five foot nine and with her long neck and strong, defined jaw, she looked something like a movie star. She wore a simple, strapless white silk dress that cut straight across the bust. A band of tulle extended the bustline an inch higher. She wore a hat that was little more than a silk bow, with a veil that fell on either side of her head to just past the elbow. In her hand she carried a long satin ribbon tied with white orchid blossoms. Though all her life friends had told her she ought to go to New York City and become a model or even an actress, my mother had never considered it. But today, looking at herself in the mirror above the fireplace mantel, she felt beautiful. She had a heart-shaped face, perfect lips, and a tiny nose. And today she was a bride and this would be the happiest day of her life. She told herself as much, as she looked at her reflection. "It will be," she whispered. "You'll see."

My father wore a black suit and a narrow black tie. A white carnation was pinned to his left lapel, its green stem wrapped in white satin ribbon. He appeared stiff and uncomfortable, a guest at somebody else's wedding. But in his eyes was a glint of something everybody mistook in the future young minister for *the spirit*. But what flashed in those eyes had nothing whatsoever to do with God.

Both sets of parents, a couple of family friends, a flower girl, and a minister. The brick house held the heat all day and the guests were hot enough as it was. If more people had been invited, the room would have been unbearable.

In the overheated kitchen, Lucille mopped the sweat from her brow with a dishrag, then tucked it back under the apron string knotted around her full waist. She added a splash of rum to the punch, then thought about it and added some more.

Lucille had worked for the family since my mother was a baby. She had a family of her own, back yonder on the other side of the railroad tracks in the little shantytown where all the Negroes lived. But my mother considered Lucille part of *her* family, not belonging to a husband and children of her own.

My mother's mother had pulled her into the bedroom before the ceremony began and whispered, "Now, Margaret? You're doing the right thing. John is a fine young man and you will be very happy."

Lucille had pulled her aside, too. She'd hugged her to her ample bosom and whispered into her ear, "Child, I am gonna miss you. You make sure he treat you right, you hear?" She didn't say to my mother that there was something funny in the young man's eyes, something not quite right. Best to keep that to herself.

My mother had to bite the inside of her cheek to keep from crying and spoiling her makeup. She nodded her head and whispered, "I will."

After the minister pronounced them man and wife, my mother and father posed in front of the wedding cake, three tiers, white frosting with white flowers. My mother cut the first slice and my father reached down and broke away a corner, stiff with frosting. As he placed the morsel in her mouth, my mother reached up with her hand and let her fingers rest on his wrist. She could feel his pulse racing. The frosting was so sweet it seemed to burn her tongue.

"After it was all over, we posed for photographs. Really, the only thing that had changed was that I now had a band of gold on my left hand. But it seemed to me that *everything* was different, even the air. It was thicker, somehow. And I felt so far away, as if I'd traveled. We were in the same room, with the same people, in the same clothes, and yet I felt so removed. I reached down and placed my hands on the little flower girl's shoulders. Her hair smelled like Johnson's Baby Shampoo and I just wanted to cry. I wanted to lean over and whisper something to the flower girl. I wanted to warn her. But of what? What would I have said? So I just stood there and I smiled and your father stood next to me and he smiled, too. And we were married and all the windows were open but the smell of flowers was so thick and sickly sweet, I felt like I might choke to death."

My mother closed her eyes. "Mom?" I said. "Are you okay?"

She turned around and pressed her cigarette out in the ashtray she'd set on the dining room table. "It just makes me sad to think back, that's all."

"But he became a minister, right?" I asked, veering away from the wedding, trying to steer her from the sadness.

"Well, yes," she said. "He was a Presbyterian minister but only for a short time. Your father decided after a bit that he didn't believe in God. And that's when he went back to graduate school and became a philosophy professor."

I wondered again what it meant to be a philosopher. I could spell the word but I could not define it.

I'd asked my father, over and over, "What does it mean?" And he'd said, "Son, it's too complicated to explain."

"What is a philosopher?" I asked my mother now.

"Oh, that's something you should ask your father," she said, as she drifted away from her easel, ambled over to the sofa, and sat.

I followed her. Images of my father were swirling in my head, down on one knee proposing, lifting a gun to his forehead. I'd heard the story of how my parents met a million times but suddenly now, I only wanted to crawl under the coffee table and curl up. I thought of her wedding cake, how pretty it must have been, encrusted with flowers made of frosting, ropes of creamy white. "And the cake was really good, wasn't it?" I asked.

My mother hadn't heard me. She sighed and continued in a flat, lifeless voice. "Your father had so much rage toward his mother, I suppose for leaving him when he was so little, letting her daddy raise him. Or maybe he was angry that she even came back for him at all, maybe he only wanted to stay with Dandy and the aunts. In any case, he was very confused, very lost. Yes, I do think he would have killed himself if I'd said no."

She brought her thumb to her mouth and bit the nail. "After we had your brother we moved to Seattle. And it was just so gray and rainy. I thought I'd made just a terrible mistake. Here I was, married to this man whose behavior was just getting stranger and stranger and I had a little baby and I was so alone and confused."

But what had she meant, "stranger and stranger"? I asked her.

"Oh, he would drink. He would sit in the dark and he would drink and then he would say things that didn't make sense. He would come into the bedroom and wake me up. *'Margaret, Margaret,'* he would shake me awake. And then he would speak just gobbledygook. He'd be frantic, very, very upset. Very drunk. And just carrying on. I was terrified."

The pines surrounding our house were so thick the needles trapped the growing darkness in the living room. My mother's form was perfectly still on the sofa where she sat now, holding her brush. Dull yellow light from the kitchen fell into a rectangle on the floor outside the doorway and then died there.

"I was very afraid of your father back then. I had this little baby that cried all the time, he cried so much. No matter how much I hugged him and tried to comfort him, he just cried and cried."

My brother, something off about him even then.

Her voice sounded like it was coming from a different room. Disconnected from the unmoving shape on the sofa. A ventriloquist's illusion. It made me uneasy, the way she could vanish from a room without even leaving it.

"After we moved to Pittsburgh, I thought I would kill myself. Your brother was seven and he just didn't fit in at school, he would come home in tears because nobody wanted to play with him. And then I would cry because I didn't know what to do. Your father was worse, he was so angry, he had so much rage in him that he kept bottled up. I thought he might snap and kill me, kill your brother. I was just terrified. Calling Mother on the phone and weeping, begging her to come stay with me. 'Margaret,' she said, 'he's your husband now. You take care of him.' I didn't know what to do. I didn't have a single friend except our upstairs neighbor, an elderly lady named Eloise but, of course, what could she do?

"I didn't dare think about leaving your father. I knew if I did that he would come after us. That he would hunt us down and that would be it. So I stayed."

She finally looked at me, sitting on the floor at her feet. Her eyes were moist.

"And then you were born and I was so happy. You were such a good, easy baby, you never cried. I loved you so much and I knew I couldn't kill myself because you needed me."

A ringing in my ears. In the silence of the dark room, it was a buzz, a steady hum, like steel stretching. It could have been an alarm of some kind, a warning issued from within.

I STOOD IN the center of the house, the only area that could not be called a *room*. It was the point at which the hallway met the top of the stairs, just at the entrance to the living room and dining room, right at the doorway to the kitchen, beneath the twenty-foot ceilings. I stood there and called out in my loudest voice, holding the note in my throat so that the word became a howl, a cry, *"Dead!"*

My mother appeared from around the corner, wiping her hands on the thighs of her skirt. Her face was stricken.

"Dead!" I called again, lifting my chin up, releasing the word like a swarm of bees.

My mother reached down with both hands and gripped my

small shoulders. "Why are you saying that? What is it? What's the matter?" There was a frantic edge to her voice, confusion mixed with terror.

Her intensity frightened me, as did her confusion. "What?" I asked.

"Why are you shouting 'dead'? I don't understand."

I looked up at her and said, "I'm calling for my *father*."

It was magnificent, her sudden comprehension, the way simply understanding rearranged her features, seemed to drain some kind of *awful* from her, some kind of dread. I saw relief in her eyes, and something else, a glint of wit? "But do you hear how you pronounce that word? You add an *e*. You are calling *dead*, d-e-a-d, not *dad*, d-a-d."

I blinked. It was impossible. "I what?"

"All these years," she said, "I hadn't realized it, not until just now, when I heard you call for him. But you do, you pronounce *dad* as *dead*."

"But how do you say it?" I felt anxious, something close to panic. Was it true that I called my father *dead* and didn't even know it? Was it possible something coming out of me could be so terribly, terribly wrong and I didn't even know it? "How do you say it?" I asked again.

"Well, *dad*," she said, "flat *a*. Bad, sad, mad. Dad."

"Dead," I repeated. And I heard it, I did. Quickly, I correctly said, "Dad." Sad, mad, glad. No, I did not say the word like that, not ever. She was right. It was incredible.

I am the only Yankee in the family for generations. Both of my parents are from Georgia, and so is my brother. I was born in Pittsburgh, so I alone have no accent.

Dead.

My father arrived at the top of the stairs from the basement. When he gripped the banister and took the final step to join us in the nowhere area, he winced in pain. As though his shoes were filled with broken glass, as though tremendous weights were strapped to his shoulders, as though corrosive acid and not blood rushed through his arteries. "Okay, okay, I'm here. What's all this shouting? Is everything okay?" As usual, he sounded like he'd just woken up from a nap, which he probably had. In his voice, the fatigue was clear. What was it now? No doubt, he was expecting to be told that something was in need of an immediate repair—a window broken, a faucet leaking.

The year before, I was throwing rocks in the backyard and one of them hit the sliding glass door, creating a spider crack. For twenty minutes he'd stood downstairs in the dark looking at the starburst crack, not saying one word. I'd brought him down there myself, apologizing deeply. But as he stood there saying nothing, I became afraid and backed away, one tiny step at a time. Until I was pressed against the far rear wall watching him watch the glass. Finally, I turned and ran upstairs. My father remained downstairs the rest of the night. The cracked glass was never spoken of again.

It was never fixed.

He stood there now at the top of the stairs, dread on his face.

My mother and I stared at him. She explained what we were talking about, my curious pronunciation. "I don't hear it," he said. "It sounds perfectly normal to me." And was he maybe a little angry at the mere suggestion? He seemed to glare at my mother as if to say, *Why do you always have to* . . .

He walked into the kitchen, grimacing with each step. Now that he was upstairs, he might as well pour himself some tea. He pulled a glass from the cabinet and filled it with ice.

My mother walked into the living room and sat on the edge of the sofa, loss in her eyes.

I joined my father in the kitchen and asked, happily, "Do you think I have a southern accent?"

My father sighed. "I don't know, son, I just don't know."

I said, "When you were my age? Did you ever think about having a southern accent?"

He poured tea from his old brown plastic pitcher, discolored now, never washed only refilled. "I don't remember, son. I don't know, I just don't know." His voice was heavy with burden.

And I felt sad. "I didn't mean to make you come upstairs. I forgot what I even wanted."

He smiled but it was an effort to do so, as if it caused him pain, physical pain that he had endured for years. He said nothing. Then he turned and walked back downstairs with his tea.

I went into the living room and looked at my mother. She seemed in a trance, standing in the center of the room and staring at a point beyond the far wall.

She said nothing and I wondered if she realized I was standing there. Finally, she said, without blinking, "Did I ever tell you how I met your father?"

I said nothing.

"We met when we were both freshmen at the University of Georgia. It was English class and we sat alphabetically, according to our last names. He was Robison and I was Richter. Our seats were right next to each other."

"You told me the other day, when you were painting. Don't you remember?" I felt as though insects were crawling up my arms and legs. Something was wrong with her. *Wrong.* The word settled over me, a weight. My mouth tasted of dread.

But she didn't seem to hear me. "When he proposed he said

he'd kill himself if I turned him down and I believed him. I believed he was serious, so what could I do? Mother wanted me to marry him, there was so much pressure. And if I didn't, he would shoot himself in the head. So I did. I married him."

"Mom? You already told me all of this. Are you okay?" I asked.

"I'm fine," she answered, her eyes glazed and fixed.

"Here, why don't you come sit down," and I led her to the sofa. She followed like a small child and sat obediently.

"Do you want some tea?"

"No, I don't want anything." Still, she wouldn't look at me.

I left her then, sitting by herself in the living room. I went to my bedroom and closed the door, glancing at the spot where Ernie's aquarium used to be, the void occupying more space than the actual aquarium ever had.

Maybe I should be careful. Maybe I shouldn't call him dead. *It might stimulate something dormant inside him.*

I PRAYED. *DEAR God, please protect my mother. Please make her stay healthy in her mind and please make her stay home.* I caught myself just in time, because I could be punished for asking a favor of God. I could be granted what I asked for, not knowing that what I asked for was the wrong thing to want. Only God knew what should happen, so I revised my prayer. *Please, God, protect my mother and whatever you think should happen, make that happen, but please make the best thing turn out.*

The shift in direction of my prayer gave me a tiny comfort, made me feel I had prayed correctly, smartly.

And then I thought to pray for one thing more. *And God? If you would, please keep an eye on my father.*

• • •

I DIDN'T HAVE any real friends at school. I was teased some for being "weird," but mostly I was left alone. I did, however, enjoy writing plays. Every month or so when I wrote one, the teachers let me put it on in the school library. Even kids who were normally hateful to me would slide up and ask if I had a role for them. I didn't write plays about farm animals with magical powers or garden vegetables that could sing and dance. I wrote plays about mothers and fathers who fought, children caught in the middle. In one of my plays a ten-year-old girl was given up by her parents for adoption. "There's just something sour in you, little girl—always been that way. Best as I can figure it, you got combined with a seed from a lemon inside my belly when I was pregnant with you." I was thrilled when this play made so many of the girls cry and ask me if it was true that a little girl could be combined with a lemon seed during pregnancy. "Not only is it true, but I know a set of twins and one of them has a stalk of corn growing clear out of the center of her head, just exactly like a horn. Sometimes, it doesn't show until you're older."

My teachers sat me down and told me not to write plays that upset the other children, but secretly, I thought they liked this one the best.

I was bad at math and didn't seem to have an ear for languages. But I loved writing plays and skits, and this was my focus, until Damian came along.

Most of us kids had been together all our lives. It was rare to have a new kid join the school. And when little Damian showed up for class one day, the class rejected him the way the body rejects a skin graft. Damian was small for his age but really, he was small for any age. He was a tiny, thread-thin boy and he had a sweetness about him that made him an instant target. That first day, some of the older kids pretended to buddy up to him, then they led him out beyond the soccer field and pulled his pants down. I watched from a distance as they shrieked, egging each other on. "Get him! Get him!" They took branches and whipped him across his naked legs and then kicked him in the stomach.

Even though these kids were bigger, and even though I wasn't brave, I ran as fast as I could and when I reached them I said, "Leave him alone." I took Damian's hand in mine and pulled him up. I led him away, carrying his pants in my other hand.

It was a mystery to me why they let me rescue Damian. Easily, they could have ganged up on me, whipped me with sticks, too. But I knew that if they tried, I would take my own stick and I would poke their eyes out. And maybe they knew this, could smell my intent the way a dog smells fear.

I helped Damian get dressed over by the jungle gym and from that moment on, I was his hero.

I'd never been a hero before and the feeling was empty. Damian was nice enough but he wasn't bright and we could never really be friends. But I was fond of him and when anybody picked on him, I put an end to it.

My one true friend didn't go to my school because he was a couple of years younger than me. Greg Abrams lived two doors down and with his blond hair and fair skin, we could have been brothers. As a matter of fact, as far as we were concerned, we were brothers, joined at the finger by the blade of a knife and a drop of blood.

Greg was younger, but he was smarter. He knew the name of just about every bug, plant, and flower and he always had ideas.

Most days after school, we hung around together in the woods. We went exploring, following old hunting trails or trying to find bear prints in the soil. We made forts from branches and piles of stones. We rode our bikes the seven miles to South Amherst to get cold sodas from the tiny old store near the railroad tracks and, sometimes, we slept outside in a tent in his backyard.

Greg never came inside my house. Although he wouldn't admit it, I knew it was because his mother told him not to. His mother warned him that there was something wrong with my parents. He didn't have to admit this to me, I could see the truth in his eyes.

Behind our houses was a path and then a stream and then more woods and there was no reason to keep walking back there, deeper into the woods, because all you'd see was more trees.

Except once, Greg and I did just exactly this. We walked straight back, crossing the stream and then beyond. And suddenly, we came across a perfect and perfectly real little house. A shack, really. But with a door and windows and a peaked roof. It even had a chimney made out of silver pipe. The door was padlocked but when we fiddled with it, we discovered that the lock was not engaged.

We entered the tiny house and saw a platform where a person could unfurl a sleeping bag and sleep very well. There were a couple of cabinets, a window in the rear that opened and closed and locked. There were curtains.

It felt like a miracle. We didn't know what to do so we sat down on the floor in the center of the room, which was the whole house, and we thought about what to do. Should we tell somebody? Should we tell our parents?

We decided we didn't have to do anything. It was enough to know that it was there. And it was okay for us to keep our knowledge of the cabin a secret.

After this, the cabin became a regular part of our lives. We didn't spend much time inside of it, but we visited it frequently, I think, to make sure it was still there. To make sure we hadn't imagined it. We never could quite believe it was real.

Privately, I liked knowing the cabin was there. I liked knowing that if I had to, I could run deep into the woods, far from home, and not be at the mercy of nature and all the creatures in it.

EIGHT

MY MOTHER WAS in the hospital.

My father said she was there because she was "nervous" and needed "some time to herself." Two weeks had passed and I wanted my mother. Already I'd begun to worry because I could not conjure her face. What would happen if I forgot what she looked like entirely?

I spent hours in her office in the rear of the house. I was a stowaway inside her closet where boxes of her papers, her knitted cape, and belongings she'd had since childhood were stored. It was where I felt her essence was most concentrated.

My brother was on a camping trip that seemed to last for months.

It was the first time I'd ever been alone with my father. The day he brought her to the hospital, he came home and slipped into my room as silently as a snake. I looked up and saw his face in my mirror and I flinched. "Well, son, it's just the two of us now," he'd said, "I hope we'll be okay." Then he forced a smile and turned around and left. I wasn't sure what he'd meant by that "I hope we'll be okay" remark. There were a couple of ways you could think about it and I didn't like either one. I made a decision right then and there: I wouldn't think about Ernie and I wouldn't think bad thoughts. The days passed slowly, silently. And despite myself I had a terrible thought: if she died, I would have to run away from home.

WITHOUT MY MOTHER there, the house was dark. My father insisted on turning off every light to save electricity. Only the dim bulb above the stove illuminated the entire front of the house. Being November, it was dark by five o'clock.

My father roamed silently at night, checking the locks on the doors, pouring himself another drink. Or he would sequester himself in the bedroom downstairs for the entire day watching football.

In the morning, my father woke me for school by knocking on my door and calling my name in a peculiar, singsongy voice that didn't even sound like him. "Wake *up, Augusten.*"

But I was always already awake and dressed, sitting on my bed. "Okay, thanks!" I called out. I stayed in my room until the last possible minute, then ran outside and down the driveway to catch the bus.

When I returned home, he was never waiting for me at the door with a kiss, like my mother. He was downstairs in the bedroom or at the kitchen table grading papers, not to be disturbed.

Some evenings he didn't come upstairs to make dinner. I wouldn't see him at all and when I looked down the stairway, it was fully dark. On these nights, I opened a can of Chef Boyardee ravioli and ate it unheated, straight from the can.

We said almost nothing to each other. Occasionally, he stood in the hall and dabbed at his bleeding psoriasis-covered hands with the thin, worn handkerchief he always kept in his back pocket. He smiled at me when he saw me. The whites of his unknowable eyes were yellow. I looked away.

One Saturday we went grocery shopping together at the Stop & Shop. My father carried a Bic pen and a small pad with him everywhere he went. On this pad he'd written a list and ticked the items as we put them into the cart. We shopped in silence, my father occasionally pausing at a shelf and tapping the keys of his Texas Instruments calculator to determine which product was the better value. When I tossed a package of cookies into the cart, my father halted and stared at the package, the muscles of his jaw clenching. "Do not, I repeat, *do not* add things to the cart which are not on the list."

I quickly put the cookies back on the shelf. "Okay, sorry," I said, eager to have the incident behind us.

But he continued to stare at the space in the cart the cookies had briefly occupied. And without looking up he continued, "First, it will be the cookies. Next it will be crackers or some such thing. And before you know it, we'll have a cart filled with all these foods we can't possibly eat and they'll all spoil and need to be thrown away."

I nodded my head in agreement. "Yeah, you're right. I don't want them anyway, I'm sorry."

And now, he looked at me. It was a hard, intense stare. "Maybe next time you should wait in the car or just stay home. I don't want every shopping trip to turn into some out-of-control nightmare with you throwing all sorts of things into the cart and me having to then go all through the store putting everything back."

I didn't say anything, I just nodded once and set my eyes on the floor.

But at the checkout my father was suddenly very light and sociable to the clerk, smiling and making small talk about the price of corn, how it was "a terrific value" to get so many ears for a dollar. He even told her he'd started to buy gas out in Sunderland because it was almost four cents cheaper. He offered to write the name of the station on a page of his little notebook for her. She laughed and said she didn't want him to go to any trouble and my father said, "Why, it's no trouble at all. See? I always carry my pad with me." He pulled the pad out of his shirt pocket and held it up to her as proof. He licked his finger and turned the page to a fresh sheet. Carefully, he drew a brief map to the Sunoco station on Route 5. He tore the sheet from the pad and handed it to her. "There you are. Now, I hope they haven't raised the prices. I'd hate to send you all the way out there on a wild-goose chase."

I'd never in my life heard my father use the expression "a wild-goose chase." He was—the only word that came to mind—*bubbly*.

He was so pleasant and outgoing that for an instant, I imagined something had changed in him. Even his face itself seemed somehow different. It was hard to exactly put it into words, but as I watched him while the clerk rung up our items, I was amazed at the transformation, at how perfectly nice and warm and normal my father appeared. I took advantage of what I saw as a remarkably good mood and, as we loaded the groceries into the back of the car, suggested we go across the street to Friendly's for ice cream.

My father said, "Ice cream hurts my teeth." And I saw that his face had changed, once again. Gone was the kind, open expression; now his face was a mirror again. His features were completely blank, his eyes absolutely dead.

I thought of the few times we'd gone to the university together and how he'd taken me around and introduced me to his colleagues. He'd seemed like such a *dad* that I'd wondered what was wrong with me to always feel so suspicious of him. I remembered thinking how, in the light of day out in the world, my father was just like anybody's father. But as soon as I was alone with him again, *Dad* was gone and *dead* was there in his place.

Riding back from the grocery store, I realized my father was two men—one he presented to the outside world, and one, far darker, that was always there, behind the face everybody else saw.

In my bedroom late that night I thought I heard him laughing downstairs in the basement. It was a soft laugh, more of a throaty chuckle. And then he stopped and I heard nothing. I didn't investigate. I knew he wasn't laughing because something was funny. It was basement laughter. And there was something crazy about it.

BLOOD STAINED THE seat of his threadbare pajama bottoms and when I asked him if he was all right he replied, "My skin has been acting up, that's all." And when he took his jacket off after work, there were bloodstains on his white shirt.

One night, instead of grading papers, he sharpened every knife in the house. He sat at the kitchen table in the near darkness and drew the blade across the gray sharpening stone. I could hear the steel singing from my bedroom.

I was very nervous and my stomach hurt. A few times, when I wiped myself there was blood on the toilet paper. I slept with the hot water bottle and wished for my mother, wished I were thirty.

And when I woke up in the middle of the night and heard my father in the kitchen speaking a language that couldn't be real, gibberish, moon-talk, when I held my breath and closed my eyes and listened to him speaking in tongues to himself alone in the kitchen, what I wished for was to be dead.

NINE

AND THEN THE men came. It was like the rains had arrived to quench the earth at last.

The men came with their machines and within the
desert of my motherless month, I feasted on their most extraordinary arrival. We were to have a new septic system.

At first I was wary, afraid of the equipment. The bulldozer
was like a giant poisonous yellow spider tearing apart the land to
lay its eggs. Dump truck, bucket loader, an arm with a toothy
head attached that mindlessly clawed at the land—the appalling
noise these things created made me believe they were breaking
up more than just the yard; they had the power to destroy the
family.

But I was spellbound. I felt that if I could make friends with
these men, I might be able to talk them into digging a small
swimming pool for me.

Standing on the front steps, I stood up real straight and tall,
hoping to double my age by doing so. I was so shy and especially

afraid of strangers and men. But I was also completely fascinated and wanted to watch every move they made. So even though it took all the courage I had in my body, probably even the extra emergency backup courage a person stores in reserve within those bumps along the spine, I managed to remain on the front steps and not run inside and peek at them from behind a curtain.

One Mississippi, two Mississippi, three Mississippi. And gradually, I began to calm down. My heart crawled out of my skull and went back down into my chest. And when the beasts turned to look at me, I didn't even blink.

I began to appreciate the beauty of these steel machines that were under strict control. I studied them and saw that as a knob-topped lever was pulled forward within the cab, the bucket of the loader was raised up in the air. When another lever was pushed away, the corresponding blade of the bulldozer would lower and scrape. I wanted to clap my hands.

With the likelihood of attack all but removed, I was quite happy to sit and watch. After a while, I saw that this pack of men had a leader. Large in all directions, he would have cut a terrifying figure were he not enclosed within the glass-walled cab atop his machine. Even his voice was giant, as now and then his head would pop out of the window and he would shout at the others, "To the left, to the left!" or "Back it up!" The pack obeyed immediately, thoroughly.

The men took occasional breaks for smoking, mashing sandwiches into their mouths, and stretching exactly like dogs, with their backs arched, tossing their heads from side to side, sweat flying. During one of these breaks, the leader stepped out of his machine and I got a good look at him. His hair was the exact color of the dirt he scooped from the earth. It appeared he had tougher skin than normal, more like a hide. He had a thick, bristly mustache, woolly eyebrows, and green eyes that glittered like faceted stones in a tarnished setting. He was mesmerizing and I could not look away. I hadn't even realized he was staring right at me until it was too late to look away.

"Hey," he called, "you wanna sit up here?" He slapped the seat of the bucket loader.

Suddenly realizing that he'd caught me watching him, I panicked. I couldn't think of what to do, so I scurried inside and stayed away from them for the rest of the day. But I watched from my bedroom window, making sure to keep only the top of my head and my eyes exposed above the windowsill. I saw him glance around a couple of times looking for me.

I was just not accustomed to large, grown people asking me if I wanted to share in what they were doing. The moment had been thrilling, too thrilling. I had to run away, because there existed the very real danger that I would run to him, leap right up into his arms, and smother him with kisses, like some icky girl. Fleeing had been an act of self-preservation, not shyness in this case.

The next day, though, I returned to my perch at the top of the stairs. It didn't take long before he invited me up into the seat again. "C'mon, kid, it won't bite."

This time, I nodded and stepped forward with confidence. I wasn't afraid anymore, not in the slightest.

After the men had left the previous evening, I'd crawled all over their machines. I sat in the bucket loader seat and put my hands on all the knobs. I bounced from bulldozer to dump truck and wished we could keep them. I even petted the bucket loader's bucket and rubbed the dirt from its teeth.

As I placed my foot on the first step, the man ruffled my hair, then pushed me up with a surprising grip—so firm and powerful that I knew he could pull trees out of the earth with just his arms. I was tempted to let go and experience the sensation of falling, then being caught by him.

I managed to climb inside the cab and sit on the seat, bouncing once or twice. "It's neat," I said.

"Yeah?" he asked. "You like it up there?"

I did. I nodded.

"Good, then maybe someday you'll grow up and drive one."

I nodded again, but I knew I would not grow up to drive a bulldozer. It would be awful to be dirty all day like these men. I didn't say it, but at best I would keep one in the backyard, like a goat.

I swung out of the cab, stood on the top step, and decided to jump. I landed harder than I expected and stumbled, clutching my ankle. "Thanks," I said, probably blushing from my clumsiness. I headed back toward the house but paused, turning around once again. I smiled. Then ran up the stairs and back into the house, which seemed dark now that I'd been outside in the bright sun. I quickly walked back to my bedroom and went to my window to watch. After a while, I returned to the front porch.

The man noticed I'd returned and he smiled at me, hitched his jeans higher up on his hips.

I waved at him, but the small, friendly wave disguised my complete fascination with him, my confusion, the sad longing I felt when I was near him. I would have felt better being away from him, but I could not leave him, not while he was there for only a few days.

In just the two days he'd been at our house, the man had given me more attention than my father had, maybe for my entire life. There'd never been anyone to compare my father with, and suddenly here was this dirty, smiling man. And his constant glances in my direction, the easy way he ran his fingers across the top of my head, the way he invited me up into his monster, these small things hit me with tremendous force.

That night, I thought about him. I lay awake for hours, imagining myself walking down the street with him, sitting beside him in a car. I imagined him tucking me into bed at night and could almost feel his mustache tickle my forehead as he leaned in to kiss me.

The next day, I was already waiting for them on my steps when they arrived. Prior to this, I had come outside only after I heard their engines start.

Seeing me, he walked over. "Hey kid, you know what? I don't even know your name. What do I call you?"

I looked down at his shoes, and said, "Augusten."

He laughed, as though what I'd said had been funny, a joke. "Augusten? But that's a *boy's* name," he said.

Furious and humiliated I admitted, "Yeah, that's what I am."

It was terrible to see the complete shock somersault behind his eyes. He stammered, "You're a boy?"

My face flushed bright red, I just knew it, and I was so mad I wanted to bite his finger off.

He walked away.

He did not glance at me again.

I'd been mistaken for a girl before. With my long, curly blond hair and fair skin, I didn't have the rugged look people are accustomed to in a boy. I was quiet, shy, and reserved; qualities one associates with a girl. But this had been more humiliating than one of my mother's dippy poetry friends thinking I was my mother's daughter.

Though I continued to sit on the steps, determined to be

brave and not hide, he never again invited me up on his bulldozer, he didn't pet my head good-bye. I had disappointed him,
disgusted him. He wanted nothing to do with me.

I could think only of revenge. I wished I had a dress and en-
tertained the idea of putting on one of my mother's. Then I
would sit on the steps dressed like a girl and I would call out to
him, *I love you! Come give me another kiss!* And his friends would
all think I was the cutest, prettiest little thing, and they would
tease him for having a new little girlfriend. *Go on, give her a kiss.
Don't be so nasty, she's got a little crush on you,* they'd say. And then
he'd have to come over to me. He'd probably whisper through
his teeth, *Knock it off, kid.* But I'd jump up into his arms and kiss
his cheeks. I'd scream, *When I grow up, I'm going to marry somebody just like you.* It would serve him right. Oh, I wanted to play
this trick. Or, even better, I could put my hair in pigtails and
knot my shirt above my belly button like the girls at school. And
I could shout to him, *Hey, Mr. Sir? Show me your thingie again, like
before.* Then, the other guys would look at him in a whole different way.

Just like that, I was no longer upset. I sat there on the steps,
thinking up ways to get him back for calling me an icky girl.

I WAS STARTLED awake in the night by my dog Brutus standing on the bed over my body so that I looked up at his belly. He
was facing the door and growling into the dark. A deep, threatening rumble was coming from him that I had never heard before. He sounded almost like an engine, like one of the machines
that ripped the yard apart. I could feel him trembling, all his
muscles were tensed. As though he would not be able to hold
himself back from lunging for much longer.

That's when I saw him. My father, standing in my room at the foot of the bed. "Dead?" I whispered.

He said nothing, just watched.

Deeply asleep, then abruptly awake, beneath the growling dog, my father standing in eerie silence—it was all so confusing that I wanted to put my head back down and close my eyes.

"Dead?" I said again.

He turned and walked out of my room.

Gradually, Brutus sank back down to the bed, his tense, powerful muscles relaxing. But now, he was awake, on guard. He faced my bedroom door. I could not see his face clearly in the dark, but I could see his eyes clear and wet, wide open.

I'd been dreaming of fish hooks. And my father had been in my dream. I didn't remember what happened. But I knew I'd had the dream before. It seemed to me, maybe, I had the dream every night.

When will my mother be home? I wondered.

MY FATHER WAS chopping wood out back, getting ready for winter. After he had a big pile of split logs, he stacked the wood under the deck and covered them with plastic. All the ice had melted in the glass of iced tea next to him on the stump. He held the ax above his head and he winked at me and smiled, but it was his other smile.

The one he only used at night when he caught me alone. The one nobody else ever saw, except maybe my mother. Perhaps this was the smile he gave her when he proposed.

I'd never seen it before in the daylight and I didn't like it.

He brought the ax down hard and the log divided, flew in two directions at once. I could read his lips: "Very much I love you." The phrase we spoke at night to each other before I went to bed. By speaking it like this, with that smile, he was distorting it, redefining it in a way that had nothing to do with *love*.

I stood still, looking at him.

He was exhilarated. But why?

That word, again, came into my head: *wrong.* Something tightly wound within me uncoiled. It was knowledge. It was the knowledge that my father was actively missing an essential human part.

That can't be, I thought.

But it was, I knew.

WHEN AT LAST my mother returned home, she was so sapped of energy and appallingly thin that I straight away worried all her most essential qualities had been left behind in the ward. I could so easily imagine a nurse's aid seeing a dark, tangled mass on the floor and sweeping it into a dustbin, not realizing it was my mother's spirit.

I was awfully tender around her, whispering and calm. Not once did I drag her pocketbook into the room, drop it at her feet, and suggest she search the bottom for extra change for me.

I feared that if I yelled or startled her in any way she would tuck into a ball and hide under the dining table, babbling until the hospital men came and put her back in the mental wagon. I worried she might shatter before my eyes into so many silvery pieces, which could never be reassembled into my whole mother again.

My father, too, was careful around her. He paused behind the sofa to rub her shoulders, just three or four quick squeezes, when normally he wouldn't touch her. He also brought her drinks: iced tea with mint plucked from the yard. He brought her tall, sweating glasses of Tab. Sometimes, he brought her a block of saltine crackers, wrapped in their wax paper wrapper. When she brought a cigarette to her lips, he would lean forward from his rocking chair to light it for her with his silver Zippo.

On these occasions, I would then pick up the Zippo and open the lid and press the mechanism to my nose, inhaling. I loved the smell of lighter fluid, and had long ago decided that I would be a chain-smoker.

With my brother away on his camping trip, and no opera on the stereo, the house was oddly silent. I could hear boughs from the pine trees scrape their needles over the shingled roof and it sounded like mice running from cats.

I listened for cars coming down the road. For me it was a game. Saabs, for example, were easy to identify because they made a whining sound like no other car. Small economy cars sounded very much the same and it was difficult to tell them apart, but a Buick Skylark sounded nothing like a Ford Granada and the fact that I could tell them apart by sound alone made me feel somewhat superior.

Mostly, my father did the grocery shopping and the cooking. He made meals from cans—salmon formed into patties with bread crumbs and egg, fried in corn oil, and served with Jolly Green Giant corn niblets. Or tacos, which we assembled ourselves from ingredients he laid out on the counter. Sometimes, he made canned ham, instant mashed potatoes, and green beans.

My mother wouldn't eat his food. She would consume only her saltines and the occasional can of smoked oysters.

I certainly offered to liven things up. More than once I suggested a family outing to Child's toy store in Northampton or a swimming trip to Lake Wyola. But no. They were having too much fun staring at the empty fireplace.

After a few weeks of my mother's new cemetery mood, I just couldn't stand it. I finally broke down and asked, "Are you going to be okay?"

She held my gaze for the longest time before replying, "Well, I certainly hope so."

I didn't like this answer one bit. It was a question for an answer, a life jacket that might not fit.

I breathed in her scent, as though filling a near empty tank. "I missed you so much," was the only thing I could say, so I said it over and over. "I missed you so much."

"I missed you, too, sweet boy," she said.

I didn't ever want her to go away again. "I love you."

"I love you," she said, and I knew she meant it because she spoke the words from the heart at the center of her chest. This, at least, had not been left behind at the hospital.

TEN

MY FATHER WAS sitting at the kitchen table grading papers and listening to the broadcast of a distant country on his shortwave radio. *"Seis miembros terroristas de la Facción del Ejército Rojo han agarrado la embajada de Alemania del Oeste en Estocolmo, demandando que funcionarios liberen a miembros encarcelados de su grupo . . ."* I sat in the chair across from him and twisted the hem of my shirt around my fingers. "Dead?"

Without looking up he answered, "What is it, son?"

"Grover has a growth in his mouth. It's in the back, on his tongue, and it's big." Even though Grover was not allowed indoors, I snuck him inside sometimes, because it didn't seem right to divide the dogs—the family—into "indoor" and "outdoor." I was rubbing his belly while he wriggled and scratched his back on the rug, mouth hanging open, when I saw the growth.

"Well," he said, marking a blue student examination notebook with his red pen, "I hope it's nothing serious." He put the booklet aside and took another from the pile.

I was worried. The growth was webbed with veins, and so large that it spread over his rear molars. It created the illusion that Grover had a plump, hairless rat in his mouth and was just holding it there in the back of his throat, saving it for later.

"Can we take him to the vet?" I asked.

My father said, "We'll keep an eye on him."

I heard the crackle of gravel in the driveway. "My mother's home," I said, pushing my chair back and running to the front door.

She pulled up to the steps, climbed out of the car. "I've got a dollhouse in the back of the car here," she said. "You want to help me unload it?"

Barefoot, I walked across the gravel to the rear of the car. Turned over on its broad side was a small house. Together we hoisted it out of the car.

My father appeared in the doorway, shielding his eyes from the sun. "Well, what have you got there?"

"It's a dollhouse. Meg was going to just throw it away so I took it for Augusten."

I was flushed with humiliation and excitement. Nothing in my mother's tone of voice suggested it was odd in the slightest to bring her son a dollhouse.

"Help me," she said, lifting it, knocking the wood against the car's rear liftgate. I quickly reached for the other side and together we hoisted it out, stood it upright beside the car.

It was a three-story colonial held together with the thinnest nails. Perhaps it had once been white, but now it was filthy, the paint smeared with dirt and rubbed away in spots revealing bare wood.

My father smiled. "Well, look at that," he said, oddly pleased. Neither of them questioned the dollhouse.

"It needs a good cleaning," my father said. "Don't bring that thing in the house until you've cleaned it up."

My mother said, "Her girls are grown now, it was just sitting in the garage like trash. It seemed a shame."

She clutched her car keys and walked inside.

My father said, "Oh boy, it's hot out here," and walked inside, too.

I uncoiled the hose and turned on the water. I sprayed the dollhouse, flooding its rooms. Then I dragged it to the edge of the yard near the woods to dry.

It should have gone to some little girl, I thought. Not just because I was a boy, but because I didn't really *play* anymore.

THE GROWTH OVERTOOK Grover's mouth and he could no longer eat. "Please," I begged my father. "He needs to go to the doctor."

"Well, we'll see how he does," he said, waving me away.

Out in the yard, the four piles of woodchips delivered three years ago still hadn't been spread. Weeds were waist high. The trunk in the Chrysler had rotted away years ago because my father hadn't swept up the split bag of road salt he kept back there. The first three steps leading up to the deck were rotten; planks of the deck itself were so soft you could poke a finger through them. If he didn't do something soon, the entire deck would rot and fall to the ground. Grover had to go to the vet.

God? Please, make my father take Grover to the vet.

I needed my mother to take my side and insist that the dog be taken to the vet, but she sat on the sofa reading Emily Dickinson and penciling notes in the margins. " 'Pretty people in the woods,' " she said to no one, looking up from the book. "Isn't that a remarkable phrase? I suppose that could almost describe us."

My father was in his rocking chair reading a textbook.

Because Grover lived outdoors, I worried that something about the outdoors had caused his tumor. Maybe he'd eaten a squirrel and a bone had pierced the roof of his mouth. Maybe the tumor was a mushroom that had taken root in the dark of his throat. Now, even when I poured hot water over Grover's dry food and let it soak until it was soft, he wouldn't eat. The tumor was just too large.

I sat with my parents in the living room looking at our oldest dog, Cream, an indoor dog. "See the way she turns her nose up in the air like that?" my mother said resentfully. "She looks just like Mother."

My father hated Cream because my mother constantly compared the dog to her own difficult mother. Once when I was small, he kicked her to get her out of the way. I'd cried and kicked him in return. I was sure he'd kick me back, but he only walked away.

"Even the way she wags her tail. If Mother had a tail, she would wag it just exactly like that. There's something superior in the way she does that. She's so much like Mother it almost makes me feel ill."

I SAT IN front of the dollhouse and peered into its tiny empty rooms. I could almost feel the presence of two girls lurking over my shoulder. Thick-boned Swedish girls with long blond hair and pale, soft wrists. Their gleaming blue eyes would know every inch of this house. While I didn't know any flesh-and-bone girls like this, they felt so real. I could almost see them reaching into the dollhouse and moving a chair just a fraction of an inch, so it's *perfect*. And I began to wonder about the girls who had this dollhouse before me, if perhaps some part of them lingered within it.

Once, these little rooms had been lovingly decorated with tiny beds, pillows the size of earlobes, skillets made of iron and smaller than a dime. What games did the girls play? Did the doll parents scream at each other? Did the doll family have a dog and did it have to sleep outside? And did the doll children have a dollhouse of their own? Was this dollhouse a mirror held up to a mirror, reflecting itself back forever?

THE GROWTH IN Grover's mouth began to bleed. Rivulets of blood clung to the whiskers beneath his chin, as though he'd recently consumed a bit of prey. Grover had always patrolled the deck like a small officer. He alerted us to cars, dogs, people out for a walk.

Now, Grover lay in the shade, his back pressed against the cool sliding glass door. I discovered the bleeding when he licked my hand and left a swath of blood behind, death's autograph.

I knew if we didn't get him help soon, he would die. But maybe that would be for the best. Because his life had been no kind of life at all. Always sitting out there on the deck, watching the other dogs inside, through the glass. He wouldn't have been able to understand why these other dogs got to be indoors and have dinner in the kitchen and come and snuggle up whenever they wanted. He would have wondered why he had to stay outside, even on the coldest winter night. Maybe he even wondered if he'd been bad. Maybe the reason his tail would wiggle so fast it became a blur every time somebody opened the sliding glass door was because he thought he might get a chance to be an indoor dog, too.

Grover couldn't understand my father's awful indoor, outdoor rule. He couldn't understand it at all.

The only thing he ever wanted was to lick a person. And that's where he got his growth, his cancer, his dead lump—right there on his tongue.

The awful truth was that it might be better for Grover to be dead. For him to not *be,* than to be always on the outside.

I wanted what was best for Grover, and perhaps what was best was death. Still, I couldn't let him go. I had to find a way to get him help. And maybe I could make my father understand it wasn't right to make Grover live apart.

"Dead? We ought to take Grover to the vet right now, he's bleeding. I mean, that thing in his mouth, *it's* bleeding and bigger and worse. It's bad. I'm scared."

My father surprised me by giving me his attention. "What did you say? We *ought* to take Grover to the vet, is that what you said?"

"Yeah, because his lump is worse, it's bleeding. I just saw." Among our family photographs was one of me dressed in a jacket and tie, holding tiny Grover in my arms. My puppy, named for the Grover on my then favorite show, *Sesame Street.*

My father was seated at the kitchen table and now he leaned back in his chair. He cocked his head to the side and extended his hands before him, as though he were shaping something, a bowl from invisible clay.

"You know, son, there are many interesting and important problems associated with the notion of 'ought.' There is the problem, which each of us faces at one time or another, of exactly what we *ought* to do. Then, there is always the problem of understanding exactly what we mean by saying that something ought to be done, and whether or not we make a distinctive claim when we assert that something *ought* to be done. There is also the problem of determining what kinds of statements are relevant for the support of such obligation statements, and even if any statements whatsoever are relevant for their support. It's very interesting to consider, how best can we express an *ought* statement?" He leaned forward and placed the sides of his hands on the table about a foot apart. "People have obligations, and the things which people are obligated to do are concrete actions. Now, as far as our obligations are concerned, we know that many of the things which we consider ourselves or others to be obligated to do are things which are not, and perhaps never will be, *done*. Therefore, you see, from the fact that a certain action ought to be done, we cannot always conclude that there is a concrete action which is the action that in fact ought to be done. Many of the things that ought to be done are never done. In those cases, it will then be false for us to conclude from the fact that some action ought to be done that there actually exists some action-event which is an action that ought to be taken. I mean," he chuckled, "did you ever consider the ramifications of such a simple word?"

Grover died.

ELEVEN

MY BROTHER WAS rarely home anymore, spending weeks on Mount October with his friends, only his torn blue nylon tent between him and the wildlife I secretly hoped would consume him. He rode his Honda 750 to Georgia to visit our grandparents, built sound systems for local bands. I didn't know what all he was doing, but I was glad to have him out of the house.

At least, at first.

For one thing, there was more food in the house without him. And items I personally selected at the grocery store—cake frosting, hot dogs, Devil Dogs—were not likely to end up devoured, their ravaged packages abandoned on the kitchen counter.

Best of all, I was now free to venture into his room on expeditions and search for money and other things I might have missed on previous excursions. The downside to his absence was that I was now alone with my parents, with no buffer between us.

My brother and the chaos that accompanied him had always allowed my parents another channel for their unhappiness. Instead of fighting with each other, they could scream at him about leaving greasy fingerprints on the good sofa fabric, car parts in the yard, or turning his room into a "fire hazard."

But with him gone so much of the time, their fights soon increased in frequency and intensity, driving me deeper into my solitary world.

And I had a feeling my brother wouldn't be coming back. If ever there was a candidate for leaving home at an early age, it was he. I was allowed to hate him because he was my older brother and he deserved it. But to my parents, he seemed to stand for all that had failed between them.

Our bedrooms were almost exactly the same size, except there was a small hatchway in the ceiling of his closet that led to the attic. When I thought about climbing into the attic, it was nearly like imagining visiting another country—I wanted to go, but it didn't seem I was quite ready. I needed to be older, or have certain equipment.

I was cautious of the attic because my brother said it belonged to him and it was dangerous up there, but he hadn't said *why* it was dangerous. His warning only made me more curious.

His bedroom was white with a single bed pushed into the corner beneath the window, a nest of tangled sheets and a blanket piled on top. A soiled pillow was punched into the corner, the case long gone. There was a desk in there, a dresser taller than me. Beside his bed was a small table that supported a lamp.

The carpet was gold but you couldn't see the actual nap because the whole thing was covered with transistors, tiny bolts and screws, melted rivulets of long-dried solder. There were glass vacuum tubes extracted from old radios, clippings of wires in all colors, quarters, dimes, half-dollars with Kennedy's chiseled profile on the face. Discarded clothing was strewn throughout the room, along with magazines, books, manuals, instructions, warnings.

It was a captivating room, new on every visit, stuffed with electronic components, bullets, keys, mechanical pencil leads, various clips, drill bits, most of a 1963 Volkswagen Beetle engine, the silver wreath crest from the hood of a Cadillac.

He would have had a conniption fit if he'd seen me rummaging around on his carpet, but he wasn't home, was he? And what that filthy billy goat of a brother didn't know wouldn't hurt him, was my feeling.

I always found something new, something that could be taken and saved as an amulet or charm, fashioned into jewelry with just a length of black rawhide cord.

There were things in here I could bring to school to show people, eliciting gasps or, even better, a low-voiced, "*You* shouldn't have *this*."

Once, in his dresser, I found a box of silver dollars. I pulled each coin out of its little plastic envelope then dumped them all into an old sock. Almost forty coins, the most money I had ever had in my life. I carried the sock with me to the mall and spent all the money on candy and magazines, records, and a mood ring. At one store the clerk asked me, "Are you sure you want to spend this? This isn't just a dollar, you know, it's an old coin, it's valuable. You could start a collection." He held it out to me so that I could take it back but I said, "No, that's okay. I have lots of them." He shrugged and dropped the rare, uncirculated coin into the register.

The summer of my tenth year my brother stayed away longer than he ever had before. He was missing for weeks.

When the wind blew the screen door open and held it like a breath and before slamming it shut, I would run to the door, certain he was finally home and suddenly very excited about it.

THE PSORIASIS THAT covered most of my father's body was angry, blazing on his skin. Patches of silvery, flaking skin, raw and meat-red underneath, expanded. Islands of rash merged, creating whole continents, until his arms and legs were covered completely, as well as his chest and neck.

Only his face was spared. A small patch behind his left ear threatened to metastasize and overtake even his features.

Despite slathering himself with lotion, blood continued to soak through his clothing making him look stabbed, wounded. There were actual piles, mounds of scales on the floor beside the bed each morning. When my mother peeled the fitted sheet away from the corners of the bed and snapped it tight, a blizzard of scales filled the air.

Arthritis inflamed my father's joints, especially his knees. Fluid gathered there, stretching the skin of his kneecaps so that they were swollen, tight, and polished. He winced in pain when he walked. His pain was endless.

I wondered if psoriasis would one day consume my body. Unstoppable, disfiguring, ruinous. At night I prayed to be spared. *Don't make me like him, PLEASE.*

My mother wrote. Closed away inside her office across from my bedroom. She even had a bathroom in there, a shower stall filled with boxes of her papers. She was self-contained.

My mother's typing was ceaseless. The machine was famished. She fed it pages of onion skin paper, and it spit them out covered in text. A bell sounded at the end of the far right margin, then a swift *ker-chunk,* as the electric, automatic carriage return engaged, beginning a new line.

On her desk, empty marmalade glasses and a coffee mug with a broken handle were filled with pens and pencils. The rolling, constant clacking, the bell sounding every few seconds, the force of the carriage return so powerful that it shook her desk, the floor, the house.

HIGH IN THE black sky above my head, astronauts from the United States and Russia met in space. I watched the sky and looked for them. I imagined them floating toward one another in their plump, air-filled suits, hands outstretched for a formal handshake.

I was worried about nuclear war. I'd heard the phrase *nuclear winter* and imagined a blizzard of gray ash; black icicles hanging from the branches, breaking, falling, spearing small animals in the snow.

Russia was unknowable to me, but the name sounded jagged, like teeth on a saw blade. "Some general over there could push a button and that would be it," my father had said.

I imagined a button the color of our house, the color of dried blood. A finger poised inches above it, trembling with anticipation. When I pictured that finger, the nail was pitted, like my father's.

I hoped the astronauts, five all together, would make friends and the Russian finger would move away from the button, and scratch an ear instead.

My stomach hurt. I either couldn't go to the bathroom or couldn't stop.

I imagined the astronauts smiling behind their reflective

visors. I imagined one of them turning back to look at Earth and winking.

I stood outside on the deck, careful to watch my step because the rot had spread farther and so many of the boards were soft— you could fall right through. I held my father's heavy binoculars up to my eyes, working the focus dial with my index finger. I could see the moon, blue-white and swirled with shadows, rutted with mystery. But I could not see the astronauts. Unless the astronauts were floating in the sky exactly above the rotting deck, I would have no hope of seeing them, because our house was surrounded by tall pine trees pressing in on all sides.

I slid the binoculars off the moon and scanned the sky. Even the stars were just luminous specks, the resolving power of the binoculars deeply disappointing. I'd begged my father for a telescope but he'd said, "That's too expensive. You can see pictures of the universe in the encyclopedia."

But I didn't want to look at flat pictures. I wanted the living sky.

I asked my father, "What *is* the universe? How large is it?" And he told me, "It goes on forever. It's infinitely large." He drew a figure *8* on its side and called it "infinity." I turned my head to the side to right the *8* and tried to connect this number with a sky so large it had no end.

That was interesting. How could something have no end? And if it had no end, where exactly did that leave us? On little Earth? I wasn't sure I liked this endless sky business.

My father said, "The universe is always expanding, getting larger every second."

"But what's it expanding into?" I asked, not hiding the alarm in my voice. That the very sky above me was expanding, that everything was expanding, made me feel a sudden and powerful sense of dislocation. As if I, and not the astronauts, were floating.

If you could make it to the very edge of the universe, just before it expanded, would you face a barrier? Would you bounce back away from it, like walking into a rubber wall? What did the edge of the universe look like? At the point where it met with the nothing?

He replied, "Son, hush. Why are you asking all these questions?"

Because I had to know.

I ASKED GOD, *Please make the astronauts be friends. Please don't let there be a nuclear war. PLEASE.*

I prayed often and I prayed hard. In movies and on television, I'd seen children clasp their hands together into a steeple beneath their chins and chant, "God bless Mom and Dad and Grandma and Grandpa."

I did not steeple my fingers.

Instead, I tried to make my head empty, hollow, and then I prayed by speaking words, whispering them with my mind.

I'd always felt that God was a watchful, interested presence in my life. A friendly voice that sometimes asked, *Are you sure you want to jump off that boulder? Are you absolutely sure?* The voice warned through suggestion, asking me to ask myself again if what I was doing was the right thing to be doing. But it never scolded me. God never punished.

God, I felt certain, did not mind that I didn't press my hands together to pray. I was casual, but I was sincere.

I knew that God existed as the Correct Answer inside my chest.

I often watched Oral Roberts on television and wanted to
call and give him money. My mother never allowed this. I
wanted to give him money because I wanted him to mention
my name on TV. Even though Oral spoke of Jesus and Sin and
Forgiveness, it never occurred to me that he was speaking about
God, that same voice inside me that cautioned me against pouring hot water on my brother's head when he was sleeping. The
voice inside me, I knew with certainty, would never ask me to
fork over some cash.

To me, Oral Roberts was more related to Jerry Lewis and his
Labor Day telethon, which I watched every year, screeching
with excitement as the numbers climbed into the millions of
dollars, caught up, entirely, in the mania of the moment and all
those glorious dollars.

On religious shows like *The 700 Club,* viewers called in and
asked for favors. They asked for money, they asked for miracles.
I listened to their pleas with sadness. Why did these people have
to call a television show to ask for favors, if God was always with
me, even when I was alone in the woods?

I glanced inside and saw my parents sitting in the living
room, my father in his rocking chair, my mother on the sofa.
Though she'd closed the sliding glass doors, I could hear her
screams through the glass. "Bastard," she shouted. "Coward."
Fragments of hate, that's all I could hear. Nothing from my father. My mother's face glistened with a sheen of perspiration as
she worked herself into an athletic rage.

I let the binoculars hang by the strap from my neck and
watched my parents, thinking, *They are everything I have.* Maybe
that's why it gave me a curious feeling of hope to look at the
sky, to try to feel its magnitude. It was proof that there was so
much more out there somewhere.

I studied my father; the slender, almost feminine fingers, so intensely disfigured, as he raised the cigarette. His tongue slipped out briefly to wet his lips before he placed the cigarette between them, drawing the smoke inside his body, and defining his cheekbones by plunging the hollow of flesh beneath them into shadow. My mother had teased him once when we were at the Bonanza steak house, "John, you smoke just like a woman." He crushed out his cigarette in the ashtray and just stared at his plate for the longest time; there was the very slightest pulsing at his temples. My mother laughed at his pouting. And finally he exploded, "I'd like to just take a shovel and smash you in the face with it, you sorry bitch." This made her laugh harder.

One day, he will kill her, I thought, watching them now.

Shocked, I gripped the railing of the deck. Why had I just thought this? Why had the words entered my head as though spoken? Was this what I really believed? Or was this just my mother's paranoia, passed on to me like an inheritance?

Or, was this something I'd known all my life? Was this merely a fact, woven into the background of my existence and therefore, invisible? Until now.

I see him lumbering into her study while she works at the type-writer, her back to the door, to him. I see his thick corduroy slacks, his red-and-black check wool jacket. The ax he uses to chop wood in his hands, the handle resting on his right shoulder, the ax head shining. In one swift, assured motion, he brings the ax down the very center of the top of her head, splitting her skull in two. The halves fall away from the blade. He reaches down and unplugs the typewriter. He walks into the living room and mixes himself a drink. Carries it downstairs. Sits, again, in the dark before the television to watch college football, Florida playing California. Without saying one word, without smiling or making any display of excitement or favor, he roots for Florida, being from the South.

Looking at him, you'd never know which team he preferred. You'd never know he killed his wife.

Without realizing it, I'd backed away from the sliding glass doors and my fighting parents in the living room. A cluster of pine needles brushed the back of my neck, making me flinch. Each year, the trees grew larger, fuller, their branches advancing, hanging heavy over the deck. Standing outside, I saw my father rise and walk across the room to his bottle.

I fidgeted just a little, shifting my weight onto my right leg, the binoculars bouncing against my chest, bumping my ribs. I pressed them firm against me to stop their sway. I listened.

I was alone with the binoculars and God and the astronauts and faintly, in the distance, I heard the fine *buzz* of an engine. I held my breath to listen. The sound grew fuller, wider, as the car approached.

As it got nearer, it sounded less like a summer insect and more like an engine, not a car but a motorcycle. I saw a light bounce against the trees. The engine revved lower as it approached and now I knew for sure that it was my brother. His was the only motorcycle on this road.

The glass door was heavy and resistant as I slid it open and ran inside. Although I didn't care any longer if my father saw me with his binoculars, I still rushed to the cabinet and put them away. I shrieked, "My brother's home! My brother's home!"

A toilet flushed, then a faucet ran briefly and my mother appeared from the bathroom. Her hands were glistening; she shook them in the air to dry them. "Where?" she asked. Then she called out, "John Elder?"

"He's not *here*, here. He's coming down the road, I heard him."

My father was nowhere. Where had he gone?

"Well, are you sure it's him?" my mother asked anxiously,

her long caftan punctuating her stride like an exclamation point.

I rolled my eyes at my dramatic mother. "It's him," I said, walking across the room. I opened the front door and stepped outside. The cool concrete of the front steps chilled my feet pleasantly. The deck had been warm, the black wood having absorbed the day's warmth like a snake.

The motorcycle's engine cracked the night in half; there was the silence of *before,* the insistence of the engine in the driveway, and then the fullness of my brother *after.*

The cycle cruised up the driveway, glanced around a rut my father had been promising for years to fill, swerved around the brown Aspen wagon. My brother crushed the brakes within his fist and the cycle stopped, kicking up dirt, spraying pebbles.

"Hey," he called out to me, peeling off his helmet. His leather jacket looked wet with blackness and I thought again of the astronauts, the first time Americans and Russians had ever met in space. I thought of a mushroom cloud rising, opening to a trembling, high-tension bloom, a shock wave on the ground spreading out like ripples on a pond after a stone has been thrown. Evaporation.

He charged up the stairs, skipping the first. "What's up?" he said, brushing past me. The contact of my arm skin with his jacket skin startled me out of my thoughts.

"Nothing," I said indifferently, but I was excited. He was now home, and even if there would be no special dinner or pecan pie, the ether was changed. The molecules of oxygen in the air seemed to align themselves; the innate chaos surrounding everything seemed, suddenly, less.

He peeled off his jacket and slung it over the stairway railing before trudging into the kitchen to find something to eat.

"John Elder, please hang up your jacket so that I don't have to walk around cleaning up after you."

He blithely ignored our mother because she'd hung up his jacket as she spoke the words.

She continued to talk at him—"Where have you been? What have you been doing? Are you all right? How long are you planning to stay?"—but could extract little more than noncommittal grunts. He'd returned home as a race car returns to the pit: for fuel, to have the tires sanded, the suspension raised or lowered. He would eat a mixing bowl filled with cereal blanketed with sugar, then go to his room to change his clothes, make long-distance telephone calls, and exchange his boots. His clothes smelled like gasoline and I wondered if he was flammable.

I padded into my bedroom, sat at my desk, and picked up a pen. I drew a series of small circles, planets. And then I enclosed them within a larger circle, irregular in shape; the boundaries of the universe. *Can the astronauts see it expanding before their eyes?* I wanted to know.

A TEAR, A rip in the silent fabric of the house. "Fuck you," screamed my brother. *"Fuck you"* like a boomerang, loose in the house, knocking over lamps, ricocheting off walls, smashing glass. Even after the words themselves had evaporated from the air I could still hear them, I could still feel them and their consequences.

Instantly, everything was wrong.

An eruption of screaming, beyond angry, violent. My father's deep, furious voice—it was rare to hear him scream.

Boots slammed against the floor, the house shook on its foundation.

It was like the universe was constricting.

Suddenly, my room seemed tiny and everything in it, frivolous. I saw it could all be wiped away, like a hand across a desk.

At once I was running, my calloused heels slipping on the wood floor. I knocked against the wall, shoved off, ran again.

There they were: my brother standing near the front door, my father opposite the stairway leading down. My father's face was plum-colored, my brother's legs were spread wide, he was ready to lurch to the left or the right, tensed to lunge.

My father made a move. "Goddamn you," he snarled, teeth bared, lips peeled back. It was more of a growl than spoken human words.

My brother bolted in the opposite direction.

They circled the stairway and the central chimney behind it, my father chasing my brother. They froze when they reached their original positions.

All the while there was constant screaming, the words indecipherable. It was a dangerous noise and it packed my ears like a blaring opera of supreme violence. My mother was here somewhere on the other side of the room near the curtains. She was generating this noise, I realized. She was pleading, terrified.

I felt, *There may be a death tonight.*

My father stumbled as he crashed toward the front door and my brother standing in front of it.

And my brother made a surprise move—forward, right to my father then suddenly around him, too fast to catch.

I was screaming, too. Useless words: "stop" and "wait" and "no." It was like shouting at two dogs going at each other.

I looked again at my mother, searched her face for certain evidence—the dynamic arch of a brow, perhaps her neck taught and extended—that she possessed the power to make this end at once. But I saw only despair and hopeless resignation. There was no strength there at all, her features were wilted, her eyes so ruined with loss I had to look away. On her face she'd already lost her oldest son and seeing this betrayal made me desperate.

She had known all along that it would come to this. The day was here. Her shoulders sagged forward as though she carried a weight strapped on her back and had walked for miles, perhaps years, and could continue no more.

She brought her hands to her face, a cigarette still burning, poised between the joints of the first and middle finger of her right hand. She shook her head from side to side. "No, no, no, no, no."

I felt a clenching, a contraction, and suddenly I was crying, wailing. *Do something,* I said with my mind. *Goddamn you, Mom, do something.*

But just as instantly, there was only this: a rifle in shadows, leaning against a wall, barrel pointing down.

I saw it before me, a vision.

And then *yes.* I thought, *Yes.*

This was God.

This was how God spoke sometimes, in pictures. Words take time to comprehend, ideas must be absorbed, understood. Sometimes, God wipes your mind and replaces the contents with a single image, unquestionable, and it is the only, the absolute answer.

Gun.

I turned away and ran back down the hallway past my bedroom and into my brother's. I winced when I stepped on something sharp but ignored it. In the dark, I doubled back and turned on the light. I dashed to the closet, slid the door open. There on the left was his rifle in shadow, leaning against the wall, barrel down.

Exactly as I had seen it.

Exactly as it was shown to me.

I reached forward and carefully hoisted the rifle, making sure the barrel remained pointed at the floor. I held the gun away from me, carrying it with both hands. As if it were toxic, a wood and metal germ, and I could not have it in contact with my body.

I was afraid of the gun but I was more afraid of what was happening inside the house. The evening was closing in around my brother, narrowing and sharpening. My father would kill him. My father was drunk and he would kill my brother. His face was red and swollen, hate wafted from his skin like a stink. I had to get back in there. I ran with the gun.

Suddenly, I was standing there before them. There was silence—perfect and clean.

Everyone was watching me.

Slowly, I stepped forward. It was as though I were in a church. The moment was sacred, holy, silent. I carried the gun to my brother and I raised it up as an offering.

"*Kill him,*" I whispered. His eyes met mine and held the gaze. "Kill him," I said once more.

Nobody breathed.

Nobody moved.

The astronauts closed their eyes.

The moment was balanced on the head of a pin.

Then my brother's head rocked back a little in astonishment and he blinked. He quickly took the gun and I could see, yes, I'd done the right thing.

I hadn't known I needed my father dead until that moment. There was only a single action: get the gun. But now I knew my father had to die.

My brother had the heel of the rifle packed tight against his right shoulder, his head cocked sideways as he looked down the barrel of the gun, which was now pointed at our father. "Back off," he commanded like an officer of the law. "Back the *fuck* off."

I screamed with excitement rather than fear. "Kill him, kill him, kill him." My throat vibrated as I screamed the words, the loudest sounds I had ever made. I felt heat rise in my face as my lungs emptied and my vision began to darken.

"Oh my God," my mother screamed. "Augusten, no." As though I had the gun. As though I were the one taking aim.

Her eyes were moist and she had disowned me. "Augusten, no," she cried with such grief.

I wanted to yell back at her, *Don't you see what's happening here? We have to make a choice.*

But I said nothing because my eyes were locked now on my brother, inching forward toward our father, who continued to stand his ground. "Back the fuck off right now," my brother ordered again. Then he said, "I keep the rifle loaded."

Like a key inserted into a lock and turned, these last words disengaged our father. For a moment, nobody moved. The air was charged with a hesitant faith. Was it really over? It was as if we'd defused a bomb and could not quite trust that the threat was truly gone. Then my father broke the spell by turning away from my brother and walking around the fireplace, out of my sight for just one moment. I was afraid to meet his eyes. But when he reappeared on the other side, he didn't look at me. He had circled the fireplace and was now at the head of the stairs, head bowed as if in contemplation or prayer.

My brother lowered the gun, and I noticed it was trembling.

Our father let out a sigh and then descended the stairs, wincing with pain at each step. And then he was gone.

I realized what I felt wasn't so much relief as disappointment. I'd gone ahead and accepted my father's death. It had seemed, once my brother took the gun from my fingers, inevitable. And I found that this knowledge stirred in me a feeling that fit comfortably inside the word *hope*.

But just then, my brother took two large steps and was standing right before me. "Don't ever touch my guns again."

I was startled and looked up at his face. He was angry with me. And for some reason, this made me furious at him. "But I had to," I said. He, better than anyone, knew this to be true. How could he be mad at me?

"No, it was the wrong thing to do," he told me.

My eyes stung and I despised him at that moment, because it wasn't the wrong thing to do. It was the *only* thing to do. *I'm the one who lives here. I'm the one who has to spend every day with him. I'm the one who can see him.* "He was going to kill you," I said. "And you know that's the truth. And I didn't do the wrong thing. And you know that's the truth, too."

My brother carried the rifle with him back to his bedroom where he gathered together some clothes, another pair of boots. "When will you be back?" I pleaded. "How long will you be gone this time?" I feared he wouldn't ever come home again. He did not answer me. With his arms full and the gun tucked under his armpit, he stepped over the threshold of the front door, bounded down the stairs.

And he was gone.

He took his car this time, not the motorcycle. Now, he would travel with a roof, four wheels. He wouldn't need to come home just because of the cold, just because it was raining. He could live in the car if he had to.

Despondent, I stood at the front door, which was open wide.

I stared out at the empty driveway, dust still floating in the air from the spinning tires. *How will I live here now?* I wondered. *How will I ever be able to look at my father again?*

My mother remained in the living room studying me. For the briefest moment, our eyes met and I believed I saw relief reflected back at me.

I stepped outside on the front steps and looked up at the sky. I saw that the moon had dipped behind the pine trees, throwing their spiky, feathery branches into shadowed relief against the glowing night sky. Frogs and crickets stained the air with their musical throb and I thought again of the astronauts. I wondered, *How do they go to the bathroom?*

And then a sense of dread rose up in me like bile in my throat, acid that burned. Because what if they hate each other, the astronauts, the Russians and the Americans? What if there is only hate?

What if God was looking someplace else?

I THOUGHT IT might be a year before I saw my brother again, or perhaps even longer, which is why it was very much a surprise to see him the next day.

It was not yet suppertime and I was in my bedroom writing in the little red diary my mother had bought for me at Hastings. It had a lock on the cover and I kept the tiny brass key in my desk drawer. Suddenly, I heard a scratching sound on my window screen. I looked up to see a branch scraping the screen. No tree was close enough to my window to scratch the screen so I thought it might be my father. But then, he would only do something like this in the middle of the night. I thought maybe it was my friend Greg so I got up and ran across my room, jumping onto my bed so I could peer out the window.

My brother was standing outside. He put his finger to his lips to silence me. Then he motioned for me to meet him outside. He pointed to the end of the driveway.

I slipped on my sneakers and ran down the hall and out the front door. My brother was standing at the foot of the driveway. I ran to him. His car was pulled over, just a few feet ahead.

"Get in," he said.

I didn't ask what he was doing here or where he was taking me. I just sat still and looked out the windshield.

My brother drove down a crude dirt road near our house that I hadn't even known was there. It was a service road, used by the power company to reach the electrical lines. I was rather amazed that an entire road could exist so near my own home and I hadn't found it. *I can't wait to tell Greg about this road*, I thought.

He continued driving until we reached a clearing strewn with rocks and broken beer bottles. All over the ground were rusty beer cans, eaten away by bullets. We climbed out of the car and I followed him around to the rear where he opened the trunk. There, beside the rusting jack and a pair of jumper cables, was the rifle.

I looked up at him but he said nothing. He simply reached into the trunk, pulled out the gun, and handed it to me. "Hold this." He took out two boxes of bullets and closed the trunk.

He began walking toward the center of the clearing and I followed, a little nervous to be holding the gun but excited, too. "You have to learn how to shoot a rifle," he said at last. He walked so fast I had to jog to keep up with him. When we reached the clearing he helped me raise the rifle to my shoulder.

He showed me how to tuck it against my body and how to aim. I would have to be prepared, he said, for the kickback.

He was very serious as he explained these things. And thorough, making sure I understood each step. He showed me the safety and said, "Always have the safety catch engaged." I nodded, trying to take it all in. "This is very important," he said, pressing my finger to the safety with his own, engaging it, disengaging it. He almost seemed angry, but I knew he was not.

Even after his meticulous instructions, I was still fully unprepared for the force of the kickback, which nearly knocked me flat onto my back. I laughed, but he didn't so much as smile and my laugh died and I stood up and fired again. He placed a series of well-shot cans on a log thirty yards away, lined them in a row, and had me try and hit as many as I could. He made me shoot over and over, as light drained from the sky and cans flew off the log. I liked looking down the length of the barrel through the two little guides that formed a sort of *V* at the end of the rifle. As it happened, I had fine natural aim and could hit almost anything he set before me.

Feeling pleased with myself and invigorated by my illicit new skill, I asked my brother if we could go get Greg, teach him how to shoot, too. He said nothing but took the rifle from my hands and cracked it open to make sure it was unloaded. He engaged the safety then handed me the two boxes of bullets. Without warning, he began walking back to the car and I followed, afraid to get left out there alone.

He opened the trunk and put everything back inside, then he got behind the wheel and I climbed in, too, thinking we were going to get Greg. But before he started the engine he looked at me and he said, "You are *not* to tell anybody about this, ever. Do you understand? Not Greg, not your mother, nobody, under any circumstances." He was looking straight at me and I thought I might have seen a little sorrow in his eyes.

But I swallowed and said, "Okay."

He put the car into gear and we started driving. "Now, we're going to have to practice this, so I'm going to come back next week. Once you get good, you can't fall out of practice." He turned to look at me. "This is very important. This is not a game. This is not like singing along to your Barry Manilow records. The fact is, you aren't safe in that house anymore. You have to be able to protect yourself because I won't be around."

He drove the rest of the way without speaking. Just before we reached our driveway, he pulled over and let me out. We didn't say good-bye, he just drove away.

I walked up to the house, rubbing my shoulder where it still hurt from the rifle's recoil. But soon, it wouldn't hurt because I would get used to it. It was amazing to me, what a person could get used to.

TWELVE

IT WAS DARK.

I didn't know whether the moon was full and ripe or just a slender crescent, balanced on its side like the white edge of an eye. Out there in the woods, the trees were thick and they were tall, obscuring the sky. Even on the brightest summer day, you could see only flashes of blue. The trees were greedy, hoarding all the light for themselves at the very top of the canopy, letting only a pittance shine through. So either the trees were blocking the moon or perhaps clouds were, a layer of them like a floating sheet.

Or maybe there was no moon at all, maybe it had vanished, bounced away from the Earth. It seemed possible tonight that the universe had gone insane.

Luckily, I knew these woods. Not only did I know the path that reached from the beginning of the forest in our backyard and extended deep, crossing a stream, running behind all the homes on our street, but I knew the landscape that held the path. I'd memorized the large rocks, had used them many times as desks, cars, horses. Beneath one low, flat stone I'd dug a hole and buried my locking fireproof box. I'd placed favorite objects inside—leaves baked with fall color, the silver ring from our trip to Mexico when I was small, a collection of stamps from countries so exotic I couldn't pronounce their names. I would return as an adult and dig up the box, I thought. It was my time capsule.

I knew these woods and didn't need moonlight or any light at all to know my way around.

But terror was dulling my vision in a way the darkness couldn't.

I was barefoot and grateful for the thick cushion of moss that grew in great blankets across the forest floor.

At other times, I'd gently peeled this moss from the ground, careful not to tear it. I would hold it before me and think, *You could almost wear this.* But the moss was fragile and would break apart if you tried to wrap it around yourself. Still, it astonished me that nature had created sheets of something so wonderful and green and soft it would be all right to lay a baby on it.

I could see jabs from his flashlight cutting into the woods on either side of me. He was back there, somewhere. The light beam was like a knife and I didn't want it on my back.

I dashed to the right, through a clutch of young silver birch trees, and ran up the embankment, crouching forward to maintain speed. With his bad knee, he would have trouble with the hill. Lumbering forward, he would need to pause and massage the swollen, throbbing kneecap, catch his breath. The hill would slow him.

But when I suddenly realized the beam from his flashlight was gone, I worried that he'd cut around, that he'd thought one step ahead of me. That he was already on the hill, climbing it from the other side. What if I reached the top and he was there to meet me?

I veered back to the path then crossed it. I wanted to stop and listen, but I couldn't. Fear pushed me forward. My breathing roared in my head, as though my ears were beside a gigantic heaving machine, a bellows stoking some hellish fire.

Even though I was wearing only pajamas and had no shoes, I wasn't cold. I wasn't anything at all. I was only a blur.

When I stepped on a branch, the rough bark cutting into my arch, I just kept running. The pain exploded in my feet, then shot out the top of my head, and was left behind in my wake.

MANY DAYS AFTER school and on the weekends my best friend Greg and I would play in these woods. School, meals, and sleep were interruptions to what became our private, untamed life.

We had a hospital, located just off the dirt road that threaded our two houses together, a natural clinic with walls made of ferns and witch hazel bushes, a bed of rust-colored pine needles. A waist-high rock with a nearly flat surface served as our apothecary, where we ground dried leaves and various barks into makeshift powders, deciding on the spot what they could heal.

"And for sprains, I think this will be good. We'll grind it up and mix it with mud from the stream and then put it on the sprain. Birch bark will be for when your heart races. You'll apply a paste on the chest."

We stored an inventory of honeysuckle, gathered in spring. The dried, shriveled blossoms could be consumed whole and contained the power to revive somebody close to death.

We'd infused the ferns, flowers, leaves, and berries we gathered with healing powers. We never sampled our drugs because we were afraid of them, though to admit this out loud would have broken the spell.

Not far from the hospital was a wooden bridge, just a flat roof of thick wood planks over the brook that ran parallel to the street until it cut back and followed alongside Greg's driveway. Beneath the bridge was our rock factory, where we smashed stone against stone, looking for diamonds.

We believed that if we split enough rocks, we eventually would find at the center of an ordinary gray rock a perfect white diamond, already cut with dazzling facets. Once or twice we panned for gold with one of my mother's pie pans, but it was diamonds we believed in.

In the other direction, just past my house, was the pond. Here, we crouched down at the overgrown, blurry edge of the water and scooped clouds of pollywogs into our hands, just for the vivid sensation of feeling *life* slipping between our fingers and dropping back into the water. The pond was rife with all that was alive—cattails bursting white fluff, throaty frogs, snakes, and turtles that could take a finger. There were cunning little birds in brazen colors that flashed about like wild thoughts and perverse impulses.

The lowly majesty of a beaver's dam at the mouth of the pond amazed us, being finer than any fort we'd ever managed to construct ourselves.

When a stranger parked alongside the reservoir and went for a walk beside the water or along the path into the woods, we stalked them from a distance, feeling possessive of every tree.

•   •   •

I WAS ELEVEN and I was strong and I knew these woods. What was hunting me beneath the black sky was old and crippled, with foul skin and a bad knee that caused a limp and required frequent visits to the doctor for draining with a hypodermic needle.

WHEN I WAS alone in the woods I brought Brutus with me. I'd seen other boys play with their dogs, watched them run in the backyard, shrieking with joy while the dog chased after, overtaking them.

My relationship with Brutus was different. I carried a walking stick I'd carved myself from ironwood and I never smiled when I was alone. Why would I? Brutus followed, sometimes charging ahead to chase a squirrel or lingering over the deflated but treacherously barbed body of a porcupine.

Sometimes Brutus sat while I lay on my side and stroked his chest. "I need you," I told him and Brutus turned his head away from me. I thought, *I need him too much. I need him to be too human.* I had the sensation of colliding with a limitation.

I PAUSED FINALLY and watched the trees for slashes of light, but saw none. As my heart settled and my ears became less occupied I listened and heard nothing but the thready pulse of the night. And I sensed that the hunt was over. I'd been prey and now I was not. Prey knows this. Prey knows when it has escaped.

MY GRANDFATHER, MY father's father, in Lawrenceville, Georgia, sent us a pool table when I was very young. I liked to knock balls into the pockets, listen as they rolled inside the channel within the table and were returned at the mouth. I begged my father to teach me to play, but not once did he play pool with me. In time, the felt was shredded, books stacked on its surface, the balls long lost.

The stain that my baseball glove had bled onto the rock was still there.

At night, my father still answered, "Very much I love you." Five words.

I MUST HAVE made my way back into the house, walked into my bedroom, and closed my hollow-core door—no protection at all against a fist. I must have peeled back the covers and buried myself beneath them, nestled my head on one pillow, and placed another over my eyes. I did not wake up in the woods, I woke up in my bed. And I was confused, because it all seemed a dream. The dark was gone, the missing moon no longer a puzzle.

After dressing for school, I walked into the kitchen, the sound of my mother's typing now reduced to just a background throbbing, like pebbles continuously running through the plumbing of the house.

My father was sitting at the table, grading papers. He had a mug of coffee before him, a cigarette burning in the ashtray.

Hesitantly, I said, "Hi." I wanted to be small. I was still confused over the dream. And yet, I was aware that the bottoms of my feet felt sore, that they dimly ached.

Looking up, my father smiled and said, "Well, good morning. You better hurry up or you'll miss the bus."

It was when he looked back down at the paper he was grading that I saw the thin line of green.

A pine needle. In his hair.

I backed out of the kitchen, as though I could undo my entrance. But I could not.

After school, I met Greg at our apothecary rock. It was comforting to be with him because I never had to explain anything. He didn't ask me why I sometimes looked frightened or had dark circles under my eyes. I imagined he knew something was wrong at my house but he also knew it was not something I could ever talk about. With Greg, I could be alone without having to be alone. It was like I was with an extension of myself.

And for a while, for as long as we were in the woods together, that's all there was. There were no mothers and fathers. It was a whole other world and it was ours alone.

With Greg I was able to escape. And sometimes, more than anything else, that's what I needed.

THIRTEEN

OWN THE ROAD from our house, close enough that a human voice could travel there, lay a body of water so entirely still that the pine trees surrounding it were reflected in needle detail. At first glance, there didn't appear to be any water at all, only forest and a sudden curious chill in the air. A levy sheltered the water from breezes, so on some days the surface never so much as trembled.

White signs posted on the land surrounding the water warned, NO TRESPASSING. PUBLIC WATER SUPPLY, TOWN OF AMHERST. But the signs did not apply to me. The reservoir was mine, as were the pine trees, the path framed by ferns, and the lady slipper orchids that bloomed only in the shade. The law I obeyed was never to pick their blooms—swollen, pink, and veined, the most human thing you could find in the woods.

The town of Amherst didn't know there was a red tackle box hidden beneath the wooden footbridge. The town didn't care that the slight peninsula that extended north into the water was overtaken with butterflies in the spring. Or that they would land on you all at once like a sentient blizzard. If you stood with your arms outstretched, you would have hundreds of wings all over your body, all of them beating, pulsing. And you would almost believe that you were about to become airborne.

The reservoir was mine.

"It's twenty-nine feet deep here in the middle," I said.

"How do you know that?" Greg asked.

"Because this is one foot," I said, holding my hands a width apart. "And there's about twenty-nine of these worth of string."

I'd come out alone the day before and measured; tied a rock around my string and thrown it over the side of the raft. Really, what I wanted to do was drain the lake and see what was at the bottom. But since I couldn't, I measured its depth instead.

Greg nodded. "That's neat. Twenty-nine feet is a lot."

We ate cucumber sandwiches that my mother had made. Our fingers were wet, which made the bread soggy and fall apart in our hands. Cucumber slices slipped out, landed on the rubber floor of the little boat. "These are good," Greg said.

"I know." Cucumber sandwiches on white bread with mayonnaise—this was the taste of summer, like biting into the actual day itself.

We tossed the bread crusts overboard for the low-flying birds and saw the flickering shadows of their wings play across the ripples of our lazy wake. We paddled slowly to the shore. It was dark as we walked home and the tall grasses by the side of the road glittered with fireflies.

AT HOME MY father saw me kneeling before my mattress. I seldom knelt when I talked to God. *Kneeling is for people who aren't friends with him,* I thought. Kneeling was formal. Kneeling was for guests. You would kneel if you weren't certain. Kneeling was wanting and showing, not knowing and believing. That's just what *I* thought, at least.

But I was kneeling that night because I needed so much, so desperately. And what if I was wrong? What if kneeling was merely good manners? Like never putting your elbows on the table, the way my grandmother Carolyn taught me.

"Augusten, what are you doing down on your knees like that?" my father asked disdainfully.

I turned around as I stood up. I sat on my bed. "Nothing."

He parked his fists on his hips and asked incredulously, "Son, were you *praying?*"

The sheer disappointment on his face made my own cheeks burn. "A little," I admitted.

"Oh, *son,*" he said, rolling his eyes and lightly shaking his head from side to side. "Jesus Christ, Augusten. You're much too old for this praying business, much too old."

His eyes continued to bore into me as if the full magnitude of my dishonor was only just beginning to be revealed.

He continued. "Praying is something little kids do. Son, it's like writing a letter to Santa. Now, you wouldn't sit down there at your desk and write a letter to Santa anymore, would you? Praying is just exactly the same thing. You're old enough now where you have to understand that if you want something in life, you are responsible for taking care of your needs yourself."

Boldly, I said, "But you were a priest."

He didn't shift position, but I sensed a change, a certain tensing of his body. "Well, no. That's technically not correct, I wasn't a *priest.* I was a preacher." He waved his hand in the air to

dismiss the distinction. "Son, there is nobody in life who is going to do anything *for* you. There isn't a God in any *traditional*
sense; a man up there in the sky who grants wishes like a magic
genie or a wizard." He laughed softly, even contemptuously. "Is
that what you really believe, son? That there's an all-knowing
something or other up there in the sky with a magic wand who's
going to get you a new record player or whatever it is you're
asking for?"

I had been on my knees, moving my lips along with the
silent prayer, because what I was asking for was *that* important.

*God, please take my father away. Please make him leave. I am very
afraid that he's going to do something bad. There's something wrong
with him. And I am very worried that my mother and I won't make it.
She used to say he was dangerous and I didn't understand. But now I
do. If death is the only answer, please take him. If he doesn't hurt me,
I'm afraid I might hurt him. I've become quite good with the rifle, you
know. I'm sure you've seen me. Unless you think I'm the one that's bad
and then you can take me. I won't be mad at you.*

When I spoke to my father my voice came out low and soft,
almost a whisper. "I don't really believe in a God that gives you
new ice skates and stuff." I kept to myself that when I ate vanilla
frosting straight from the can, I could feel God standing right
beside me like a real best friend, watching and smiling and wish-
ing he had a mouth.

My father stepped forward and slapped me on the shoulder,
a rare and shocking instance of physical contact. "Okay, son, all
right," he said and walked out of my room. Without having to
watch him, I knew for a fact that as he walked down the hall and
into the kitchen, he turned off each light switch as he passed it.
He then checked all the burners on the stove, even though nobody had cooked a thing all day—I'd had cold cuts from the

package for dinner, pickles from a jar. Next, he would walk into the living room and peer at his thermometer-barometer unit, which was bolted to the wall. He'd repeat the figures in his head until he made it back into the kitchen where he would write them down on the top page of his diary. Next, he would pour himself a glass of vodka and carry it into the living room. He would sit in his rocking chair in the dark.

I didn't know if it was because of what he said or just that I was getting older, but I soon stopped feeling God standing right beside me everywhere I went. I stopped talking to him when I was alone in the woods or under the bridge looking for diamonds among the river stones. I stopped asking God to protect me.

I came to think that maybe God was what you believed in because you needed to feel you weren't alone. Maybe God was simply that part of *yourself* that was always *there* and always strong, even when you were not.

And if I put everything in God's hands, wasn't that a copout? If I didn't get what I wanted I could use God as an excuse, I could say, "He didn't want me to have it." When, in fact, maybe I hadn't worked hard enough on my own.

If I wanted to be free of my father, it wasn't up to some man in the sky. It was up to me.

THERE WERE THREE of us. It almost felt like the house contained three caves, and each of us sat in the back of our own.

Sometimes I could hear my mother howl from inside hers. Over the sound of her endless typing, I could hear her forlorn, desperate wail. Like a wounded animal crouched in the corner, knowing it would soon run out of life.

When my father came near my cave, I could hear him breathing and grinding his teeth.

People believe in God because they can't face being alone. It didn't scare me to think of being alone in the world. It scared me that I wasn't.

FOURTEEN

M Y MOTHER COULD not bear to be in the house. A terrible anxiety consumed her. She swung from darkness to euphoria. "I think I have to kill myself" could become "They want me to read my poems on the radio!" in just an evening.

When she wasn't in her office typing, she was talking on the phone or at the university meeting with her adviser to discuss her thesis, a book of poetry. Now that she was working toward her degree, she met friends for coffee at eleven at night. She went to movies she had no particular interest in seeing.

"Did you take your medication?" my father asked her every day.

The question infuriated her. The question was a switch that engaged her wrath. Per her psychiatrist's orders, she took two Mellaril, eight Valium, and three Elavil each day but still she vacillated wildly, like an electric line outside in a storm. "I'm losing my mind. It's exploding right out of my head," she'd scream, clutching her skull.

She felt we should take a holiday. "We'll take a trip to Martha's Vineyard for four days." When my father agreed to come it became a *family* trip. Minus my brother, of course, but then the four of us had never done anything together. We'd never gone anywhere together, not even to the grocery store. Even when my brother was younger and lived at home, he would hole up in his room.

It was odd. My brother had been part of a family of three, and now I was part of a family of three. We'd never been a family of four, not for long. And even though he and I shared the same parents, they were not the same *people* by the time I was born. My brother and I were truly raised in two different families, by two different sets of parents.

When he was born, they were young, smartly dressed, and freshly married. They must have still felt much hope about the future, starting a family, making a life together. A photograph of the three of them shows my father smiling, my brother eating cotton candy from a hollow paper stalk. My mother looked so young I didn't recognize her, the expression on her face so tentative and fragile.

I was born into their smoking, oily wreckage. Married almost ten years by then, my mother was suicidal and my father, suffering with psoriatic arthritis, was consumed by alcoholism.

He stopped preparing for his classes, and taught them mechanically, dispassionately, from muscle memory. He wondered if he should just shoot himself in the head. He must have wondered, too, if he should take his family with him.

I'd asked my mother, "Was I on purpose or an accident?" And she'd replied, "You were the most wanted baby in the world." But I knew this wasn't true.

Every year on my birthday she told me about the silver, blustery October night that I was born. How she'd started to feel contractions and she knew that labor had begun. "You need to drive me to the hospital now," she'd told my father. But he'd wanted her to make him some spaghetti first.

Excited people can't eat. For the entire week before Christmas I could barely keep a thing down except candy canes and chocolate Santas. If I'd *really* been the most wanted baby in the world, if he had wanted me even a little, he would have been in the car, with the heater running and the radio tuned to a station that played something to take her mind off the pain, oldies like Benny Goodman or Artie Shaw. Instead, he made her boil water in a pot. Fry ground beef in an iron skillet. Heat a jar of sauce. She grated cheese, wiped the counter clean. She left the grater in the sink to deal with later.

More than once my mother told me she'd been overpowered by my drunk father, pinned to the bed, "taken." It was vile to imagine my parents having sex, especially if my father had forced it to happen. Unfortunately, that's exactly what I believed occured.

My brother remembered when "things were more normal." He'd told me stories from *before.* Days when she made tuna casserole and planted flowers.

It was like the nuclear war I dreaded as a little boy had turned the sky from blue to gray. There were no trees and the rivers, streams, and oceans were brown, and the only remaining nourishment was expired food in dented cans that we went ahead and ate anyway. But my brother remembered cows and birds and white snow. My brother remembered the sun. That's how it felt. I recalled the photograph of him with the cotton candy, and I thought, *then.*

He got to the table first and ate all the meat and left me a pile of empty bones to pick at, to sustain myself with slivers of fat and gristle.

Still, I was excited about the "family" trip. It had only happened twice before. Once, we went to L.L. Bean in Freeport, Maine, but we drove straight back that same night, getting home at three in the morning. The second trip was to Newport, Rhode Island, to look at the mansions—my idea. And now this rare third outing.

We would leave in a week.

My father bought a map of Massachusetts from AAA. He unfolded it on top of the kitchen table, arranging beside it a pad of paper and a row of four ballpoint pens, their edges flush with the pad. At night, my parents planned the vacation and I stood between them, wiggling with excitement, chattering at them endlessly.

"Will we have lobster?"

"Will we see whales?"

"Will we swim in the ocean?"

My father's answer was the same for every question. "Son, let's just wait and see." He would guarantee nothing, the holiday had no warranty. "I would hate to promise you something and then have you be all disappointed if it didn't happen."

Gradually, I stopped wiggling and took a seat. I parked my arms on the table, dropped my head onto them. It's not that I was bored. It's that there was not enough to be excited about. The only thing I was promised was that we were going to Martha's Vineyard. I was not allowed to hope for more, so I didn't.

Soon I began to dread the trip. If my father couldn't even *walk* here at home because his knee hurt, and he couldn't play ball or even checkers because he was too tired, why would anything be different just because we were on an island?

I imagined a trip where my father sat in a chair in the motel room and smoked in the dark, just like at home. And my mother propped herself up in bed writing in her notebook, her lips moving to the words, just like at home. I imagined them getting into a fight and waking the manager, being asked to leave at three in the morning. I could see myself standing beside the car, holding on to my pillow. Geography was simply too weak a force to change my parents' behavior, of this I was certain.

My father drew on the map with a red pen, tracing the line of highway that would deliver us east across the state, then south to the coastal town of Woods Hole. He picked up a black pen, uncapped it, and carefully marked an *X* on the map. He tapped it with his finger. "Right here, this is where we'll catch the ferry." Then he placed the cap back on the pen, set it down on the table with the others, and aligned his ruler on the map. He measured the distance from our town to the black *X*, accounting for the curves. Then he read the key at the bottom of the map. One inch was equal to fifty miles. In this way he was able to determine that the trip would take us approximately three hours.

Next, he calculated the amount of fuel we would consume, which he multiplied by the current price of gas per gallon for a total of $4.86. This figure he printed neatly on the first page of his pad of paper.

He said, "We'll allow an additional ten dollars, for emergencies." I wondered what would constitute a *ten-dollar emergency*.

He said that if we left by seven in the morning we wouldn't need to stop along the way to eat.

With each mark of his pen, each measurement of the ruler, it was as if, inch by inch, he was removing any chance that something unexpected might happen. Like lunch.

I developed a rank, metallic taste in my mouth, always the

precursor to illness. My throat felt raw, like I'd been howling. And my joints ached, my skin tender to the touch.

Sickness was how my body responded to anxiety.

WE STOOD ATOP the cliffs at Gay Head on the southwestern tip of the island. My father, closest to the edge, took expansive breaths. He scanned the horizon, his right hand poised against his forehead to block the sun.

I stood behind him on his left. I watched him.

My mother hung back behind us both, her arms crossed protectively across her chest. She smoked, exhaling curling wisps of smoke through her nose, her face to the sky. When she glanced down again, it was not out at the view, but rather at the earth around her; at ruddy gravel stirred by countless feet, crushed grass, tiny trampled wildflowers, pull tabs from beer cans. She turned and walked away from us, her attention on the very near and ordinary, not the distant and grand.

My attention shifted between my parents—my father watching the horizon line, dreaming perhaps that he was a sea captain piloting a clipper ship, his ancient wish, and not a man looking out to sea from shore, and my mother lost in whatever thoughts and images had been sparked by the path, the grasses and stones.

My mother existed largely in the past, replaying her south Georgia childhood at different speeds. Perhaps the scattered peanut shells I saw around me at my own feet reminded her of pecans and her beloved father's orchard. Or maybe everything reminded her of her chilly Victorian mother, always withholding, punishing. A Latin teacher who warned, *Aut disce aut discede,* and *Non semper erit aestas.* Either learn or leave, and It won't always be summer.

This moment between them was like so many others. I was there, yet I was not. I occupied the space physically, but none of their attention.

I wondered if I screamed would they both turn suddenly and look at me? Or would they be unreachable? I had screamed before and not gained their attention. I had tried and tried to get them to see me.

If I wasn't an accident, if my mother *was* telling me the truth, wasn't this worse? If I wasn't an accident, mustn't I then be a crushing disappointment? My father couldn't bear to be with me, it was as if to do so caused him more physical pain than all his ailments combined. And my mother lived in exile within her own mind, devoted only to the past.

My brother enraged them. With his wild life, his greasy hair, his disregard for the seat belts of life. With his requests for money, his thanklessness when they gave it to him. With his be-littling nicknames for them—"Slave" and "Stupid"—to which they responded resentfully but thoroughly.

My mother's form was farther away now; if I called she would not hear me.

It was late afternoon and we were facing west. The sun was so magnificent that I realized at once how, at home, I was de-prived. The pines we lived inside of insulated me from the sky, the sun. There was a vastness in the outside world. There was more than I had at home. There was everything.

All at once, I wanted to live here, on the beach, near the sea. I felt the freest I'd ever felt just standing there. And this made me think of my brother, leaving home so young. Was this what he felt like? Was this what he saw? I understood why a person would want as few wheels as possible, no doors, no roof, no place to store a suitcase or anything else from the past.

The back of my father's head was larger than the sun, twice the size at least. He stood no more than three feet from the edge of the precipice. He had not glanced back at me once. I reached for his hand. He withdrew it and slid them both into his pockets.

My mother was out of sight.

I took one step forward, then another step to the right, and finally a third. So that I was now standing directly behind my father. I inhaled through my mouth, tasting the salt, his Old Spice cologne, and something else—the atmosphere around the sea, the waves themselves.

We were entirely alone, my father and I. We were alone together. We were an *Us*.

For my twelfth birthday just the month before, my parents had given me a book, *Where Did I Come From?*, which explained the mechanics of life. Though I already knew the basics, I'd realized, reading the book: there are no exceptions. *His* ejaculation had created me, *his* orgasm resulted in the fact of me, standing there behind him. One erection, a number of thrusts, a release. And there I stood.

I stepped closer.

And I sat on the ground. Small pebbles, sharp edges of stone pricked me through the seat of my pants. I placed my hands beside me but it hurt, so I wiped the area clean of stones and then tried again. Now my hands rested on firm, dry ground on either side of me.

The sun streamed between my father's legs and shined in my eyes.

I raised my legs off the ground, I took a deep breath, I lined the bottoms of my feet up with the meat of my father's calves.

I kicked.

There was a gasp of surprise, then the guttural wheeze of air escaping from the bottoms of his lungs. His body folded and he collapsed right there on the ridge.

It was very fast.

His tailbone smacked the ground. I heard it break. It was a sound I'd heard before, which surprised me. It was the sound of a dog cracking into a T-bone from a steak.

And my father was gone.

I blinked. I stood.

I took two large steps and I peered over the edge of the cliff, saw my father sliding down the vertical earth on his back. He bounced. Desperately, his arms scrambled, grasping uselessly at grasses that released their hold.

I screamed, "Dead! Dead!"

I opened my mouth and my throat and I made the loudest sound I had ever made or ever heard. Even as the scream left my own body, I felt in awe of my ability to sustain the note. There was a beauty to the scream, it was something of an accomplishment. I was like a lighthouse standing there on the cliff, my voice a warning to all the ships at sea.

I turned and saw my mother running up the road. She stumbled and recovered, her arms flailing out at her sides, gravel sputtering at her feet.

I leaned over and looked again down the cliff. My father's crumpled body lay at the very bottom on the beach. He was shaped like a horseshoe. He looked like a baby and I was overcome with the desire to cradle him, to pick him up and cradle him in my arms, to kiss his forehead. I looked away.

I ran toward my mother, fell, got up, fell, got up. My face was wet—I hadn't realized I was sobbing. I felt the finest joy, a note of pleasure and release, entirely new.

I was hysterical. "Mom, Mom, hurry, oh my God. My father,

he got too close. He stood too close to the cliffs. I told him to stand back." I screamed this line again: *"I told him to stand back."*

My mother was murmuring, "Oh no, oh no, no, no." As she reached the cliffs, she grabbed me by my shoulders, threw me in the opposite direction, away from the cliff, as though it could willingly inhale, suck me over, too.

She threw me hard against the ground and this dented my heart. It was the truest expression of love I had ever been shown.

She stood at the edge, looking down. She brought her hands to her face, covered her features. She screamed through her fingers, took a step backward, then another and fell to her knees. Still, she, too, was close to the edge of the cliff, but not perilously close. She did not take that risk.

"We have to get help," she said, looking up at me through her fingers, her face ruined, rearranged by shock and grief. And was that not excitement that I saw flashing in her eyes? Was there not joy there, too?

"Call the police," I shouted. Knowing, of course, she had no more access to a telephone than I, out here on the cliffs at Gay Head point, so many miles off the coast of Massachusetts, alone in the Atlantic Ocean, beneath a fine, feathery layer of cirrus clouds, at the distant edge, and not the center, of our galaxy.

My mother had seen him standing there. She would tell the officers, "He was watching the horizon when I went for a walk. I saw some shells on the ground and I wanted to collect them." Later she would admit, "Yes. We've had some problems, we argued like every married couple." Finally, she would acknowledge, "I suppose you could say he was depressed."

I would weep, withdraw into myself. The officers would not press me, a twelve-year-old boy with blond, curly hair and an upset stomach, holding his mother's hand and wiping his nose on his wrist.

He slipped, *of course*. It would be obvious what happened.

How else could he have landed there at the bottom with the waves? There wasn't another person around for miles.

There had been only two people on that cliff. A man and a boy. A father and his son.

EACH NIGHT, I lay in bed replaying the fantasy. Wouldn't it be just that simple? Wouldn't the police truly believe it had been an accident? I really could get away with it, couldn't I?

As long as nobody was there to actually see me push him, nobody would even consider that I had. Who would blame a twelve-year-old?

With my father gone, I might have a chance. As long as he was alive, as long as he was there giving me nothing of himself, I had to fight. I had to swallow the terrible truth of his disinterest and tell myself it didn't matter.

I was seeing the enormous energy it took to not hate him. It would just be such a relief.

But when I finally felt I had every detail worked out perfectly, I understood that I could never do it. I could not end his life.

To do so would be interfering with God, whatever God was. Even if there was no God, it was still not my decision to make. Killing him would offend nature itself, defile the fact that he had spontaneously appeared in the world. And besides, killing him would not make him love me. It would not free me. I would be like my mother, trapped in the past, living within this single terrible act for the rest of my life.

If he'd beat me, if he'd tortured me, maybe then I could do it. Yes, then, I thought I could.

All he was guilty of was not wanting me.

That was not worth a stain on the fabric of my past, one I

would never be able to wash out and would have to hide from everyone. If I killed him, he would continue to rule life.

It never occurred to me that while I was engaging in this elaborate fantasy, my father might be entertaining a fantasy of his own. Only in his, it was I who was standing on the cliff's very edge looking out to sea, my mother right beside me. While he stood behind us both, smiling and doing just a little bit of probability reasoning in his head.

IN THE END, my father didn't come on the trip. My mother and I went alone. She wrote in her black notebook and I walked along the chilly gray beach. The clouds were not wispy, as I had imagined, but dark and pregnant with rain. We stayed for two days, not four. At Gay Head point, I wondered what it would feel like to fall.

If you raised your arms above your head like you were diving and you aimed true for the waves, wouldn't you experience perfect freedom? That the body would land broken on the rocks below didn't matter, because you wouldn't be there for the landing. So you would experience only that single moment of clean, pure freedom and grace.

But then, that would be it. There would be no chance to remember that feeling and strive, for the rest of your life, to feel it again. Or to surpass it. Or to pull somebody aside and tell them what it had felt like.

There would be nothing. It reminded me of when I wanted to find out about the universe and I'd asked my father, "What was there before there was everything?"

He said, "There was nothing."

"But what is nothing?"

"Nothing is nothing," he said.

It was so difficult to picture. Because wasn't nothing something, too? Wasn't the thick silence and blackness of nothing actually a place you could be?

Son, I'm tired. Please just go outside and play.

Is that what death was like?

But no, it wouldn't be "like" anything.

I was desperate to discover what *nothing* felt like. It was the *absence* of *something* that attracted me. It was the start. Everything important originated with nothingness.

At Christmas, the floor could be spread with gifts, but I would be concerned only with what I didn't get. Not pouting because I didn't get a sweater vest, but wondering, *What would have been in the box that isn't here?*

My brother inspired awe in me because he wasn't *there* anymore.

I loved my mother most when she was locked behind her door, writing. Because I couldn't have her. And because I never hugged my father, it was his embrace I sought most of all.

Where there is nothing, absolutely anything is possible. And this thrilled me. It gave me hope.

In a way, if I wasn't having a happy childhood right now, I could have one later.

I knew I had an ugly life. I knew I was lonely and I was scared. I thought something might be wrong with my father, wrong in the worst possible way. I believed he might contain a pathology of the mind—an emptiness—a knocking hollow where his soul should have been. But I also knew that one day, I would grow up. One day, I would be twenty, or thirty, or forty, even fifty and sixty and seventy and eighty and maybe even one hundred years old. And all those years were mine, they belonged to nobody but me. So even if I was unhappy now, it could all change tomorrow. Maybe I didn't even need to jump off the cliff to experience that kind of freedom. Maybe the fact that I knew such a freedom existed in the world meant that I could someday find it.

Maybe, I thought, I don't need a father to be happy. Maybe, what you get from a father you can get somewhere else, from somebody else, later. Or maybe you can just work around what's missing, build the house of your life over the hole that is there and always will be.

FIFTEEN

MY MOTHER AND I returned from Martha's Vineyard with sand in our hair and shoes. On the drive back, she had said almost nothing, fixing her gaze on the highway, her lips moving along to words only she could hear.

Only once did she speak to me, saying, "Hand me my bag from the backseat."

I pulled the sagging brown leather purse between us and unbuckled the flap. Without taking her eyes off the road she rummaged through it for a bottle of pills. She handed it to me. "Would you please count out three of these?"

She swallowed them with the dregs of the coffee in her white foam cup.

When we walked in the front door, dragging our bags against the gravitational force of reentry into the denser atmosphere of home, vacation over, I was surprised that Brutus didn't come running to greet me.

This wasn't normal. Brutus should have barked twice, leaped over anything in his way, and barreled to the front door, nearly knocking me over with the vigor of his rottweiler joy.

"Brutus!" I called. "Brutus, come here."

My mother withdrew to her office, closing the door. The typing began almost immediately as she put on paper what she'd been writing in her head during the drive home.

I wandered into the kitchen, then the living room and through the dining room. Where was he? I walked out on the deck to see if for some reason he was outside, but I didn't see him. Glancing down, I saw the rot had spread to the sliding glass doors. Now, anyone who stepped outside on the deck risked falling through. The wood was cracked, splitting. I bent down and poked my finger into the wood—it went deep. The whole deck would need to be replaced. And all it had ever needed was a coat of stain.

What had Grover needed? Probably something just as small. A certain vitamin, a protein missing from his diet. Or maybe he only needed somebody to stop him from eating something wild and dead, diseased, infected, contagious.

I missed him.

I missed Ernie.

Could Brutus be downstairs in my parents' bedroom? I ran down the steps, opened the door to their bedroom, heard the television.

My father was propped up in bed watching a game on the black-and-white television and Brutus was on the floor beside the bed.

"Hey," I called out. "Here he is."

My father said, "How was your trip?"

I told him, "It was fine. It was good. Nothing really happened, though."

"Where's your mother?"

"She's upstairs. She's writing."

I took another step toward the bed and Brutus sat bolt upright, the fur along his spine becoming erect, as if injected with air. He growled, his lips curling back to expose his ivory teeth.

My error was assuming Brutus had mistaken me for an intruder. "It's me, Brutus," I said. "It's *me*." I took another step forward, reaching for him to scratch behind his ears.

He snapped, ripped a chunk from the air in front of my hand and I recoiled. "Dad," I cried, "what's the matter with him?"

Now the dog was standing, his back parallel to the bed, his head turned to the right toward me. It was as if he was guarding the bed, blocking it with his body, but making it clear that he would, if necessary, turn to face me head-on.

Without looking away from the television, my father said, "Don't go teasing the dog. He doesn't like it."

I backed away. "I'm not *teasing* him, I didn't do anything to him at all. I just came down here and said hi to him and now he's threatening me."

"He doesn't know you're only playing, he's just telling you he doesn't like it."

That night, Brutus did not sleep in my bedroom, like he always had. He slept downstairs with my father.

While my mother and I were on Martha's Vineyard, the dog's allegiance had shifted from me to my father. Now, he followed my father from room to room. When my mother or I approached him, the beast stood, hackles raised, and growled.

Just a couple of days after returning, my parents had a big fight in the kitchen. My mother began shouting and Brutus backed her into the corner against the cabinets. My mother screamed, "Call him off, make him stop," but my father said nothing, he only smiled. Then he laughed as she began to cry, genuinely afraid as the dog rumbled like an engine and the lip of the kitchen counter pressed into her lower back. It was one of the few times I could remember hearing the sound of my father's laughter fill the house.

THE DOG WAS now a menace and had to be watched. My mother and I began to plan carefully when we needed to leave our rooms. If I went into the kitchen for a drink, I would stop into her office. "It's clear, they're downstairs." And she would take advantage, run into the kitchen and bring three drinks back to her office with her, saving later trips.

If my father and Brutus were in the living room, we would stay entirely away from that end of the house. There was a prowling dark force in the home now, a set of snapping jaws to be avoided. My father enjoyed a new sense of power, he was untouchable. My mother stopped screaming at him; I left him alone, didn't hunt him down and pester him with my questions or ask him to play with me. Brutus not only guarded his body, but his privacy.

I wondered how my father accomplished this, how he turned the dog against us so swiftly and completely. It was like a magic trick.

I STOOD ON the deck watching my father split logs. He worked until he achieved a pile, then he parked the blade in an upright stump of wood. He removed the square, white handkerchief from his rear pocket, unfolded it, and mopped his brow.

"Excuse me?" A student crunched through the woods

between our house and the Allens' next door. Last year, the Allen family moved, leasing their house to graduate students from the university. My father complained that the students parked too many cars in the driveway, left bags of trash in front of their garage doors, played their music so loud we could hear it next door.

Brutus, who had been napping beside my father's pile of split logs, suddenly came to attention. His ears tensed to locate the sound. Instantly, seeing the unfamiliar young man exit the woods, Brutus galloped toward him.

"Mr. Robison, I need to speak with you about your dog. He's been coming into our yard and threatening us." He stopped in his tracks when he saw Brutus heading toward him.

Brutus froze, hunched forward. The hair along his spine was ruffled into a comb.

"Can you call your dog off, please?" the man shouted impatiently.

Brutus became more agitated hearing the increased volume of the man's voice. His growl became more threatening, no longer just a rumble from his chest, and now his teeth were exposed.

My father did not call the dog off. "Well, maybe if you didn't let the damn trash pile up in front of your house the dog wouldn't come over there in the first place."

"Call your dog off, please," the student said, his voice pitching higher with anxiety. He took a step backward and that's when Brutus sprung forward.

The man shouted when Brutus lunged, his front paws easily topping the man's shoulders. He snapped his jaws in the man's face.

"Dead, call Brutus, call Brutus!" I screamed. "Brutus, *no!*" I shouted uselessly from the deck.

Brutus shoved the man to the ground and was standing on top of him, snarling and snapping, making hideous noises. I was certain that he was biting the neighbor, shredding his neck.

Still, my father would not call off the dog. It was like he wanted to see what would happen. That's all. He just wanted to watch.

"Dead," I screamed. *"What are you doing?* Dead!"

Finally, my father called the dog. "Here Brutus, come here, boy." And Brutus whipped his head around to face my father. "Come here, Brutus," he said again and Brutus obeyed, stepping off the neighbor and running to my father's side.

The neighbor stood up, running his hands across his chest and checking his hands for blood. There was none. He ran his fingers across his face, his cheek. He shouted, "Jesus Christ, that dog is insane, *you're* insane. Why didn't you call your dog off? He could have killed me."

My father said, "I wish he had killed you, you son of a bitch." And then he walked over to stand just a foot in front of the neighbor. "I have had it with you, frankly. You and those damn kids have turned that house into a real dump. With your garbage bags and your loud music and now you come over here complaining about my dog? I'll tell you what, young man. You come over here again and I won't call my dog off. You hear me, young man? Next time, I won't call off that dog."

The neighbor briefly glanced up at me and I had to turn away I was so ashamed.

THAT EVENING, MY parents sat in the living room and talked about the dog. As his fate was decided, Brutus slept in oblivion at my father's feet.

"Aw, that would just make me sick," my father said, "just *sick*."

My mother was insistent. She argued that there was no other option, the dog's character had changed. Perhaps there had been latent aggression that was only now being expressed. Whatever the reason, the dog had to be put down. "Damn it, John, it's unsafe to be in the same house with that animal."

"Christ, Margaret, you make that damn dog sound like an unholy monster. He's not going to attack you or Augusten, for crying out loud. Augusten just has to learn not to tease him."

"Augusten doesn't tease him, John," my mother said incredulously.

Until now, they hadn't seen that I'd entered the room and was standing on the other side of the fireplace, listening. I spoke up. "I *don't* tease him, Dead. He just growls at me whenever I come near you." I advanced into the room and, as if to illustrate my point, the dog emitted a low growl.

My mother pointed to the dog. "John, do you see? Do you see that? He's growling right now. We can't live this way anymore."

Resigned, my father acquiesced. "Oh, Christ. All right, all right. I'll have the damn dog put down tomorrow morning. I just think it's a real shame that the two of you hate poor Brutus so much."

I'd adored Brutus. He used to sleep in my bed with me and stand guard over me and I'd never felt so safe. Then we went away for just a couple of days and he'd become some sort of thick-necked devil, my father's henchman.

But then, how had he accomplished this? How had my father essentially brainwashed Brutus, taken complete control of his mind, in the space of a few days? Somehow, I didn't think

Milk-Bone dog biscuits would quite do it. No, my father had to have employed another method of training. Something that would make Brutus learn *very fast*.

Electricity? A car battery? Or perhaps the fireplace poker? What had my father done to the dog?

I had a hard time falling asleep that night, thinking about this, and what would have happened if Brutus had done more than just pin the neighbor on his back. What if he really had ripped into him? And why didn't my father call him off?

True to his word, in the morning my father drove Brutus to our vet, just down the street. He came back with Brutus's collar and he placed it in the center of the kitchen table, like a bowl of fruit. It was our punishment.

THAT EVENING I heard terrible noises from my parents' bedroom in the basement. My mother screaming, my father's most frightening monotone, not a decibel of emotion in his voice. I had always found his silence more alarming than her cacophony.

I raised the volume on the small television and concentrated harder on the picture. But finally, I couldn't stand it any longer and I had to go downstairs to investigate.

I thought my mother must have been shouting into her pillow, because I couldn't make out any words. My father begged for something. What could it be? The tone of pleading was unmistakable in his voice. Was he asking her not to kill herself? Was he saying, *Don't leave me?*

I heard my mother gagging. And then she was coughing, spitting.

"You fucking bitch," my father said. Hateful, ugly. It was

shocking to hear. Like putting your ear to a shell to hear the ocean and instead receiving a bite.

My mother wept. "John, please. Please let me *be*."

Suddenly, my father was shouting. "You wanted the dog dead, I had him killed. Goddamn you, why won't you ever show me a little fucking gratitude."

The sound of my mother's crying warbled, she moaned miserably. "John, *please*," she begged.

I heard the springs of their bed creak, then a frantic, rhythmic squealing from the mattress as though it were screaming. My mother's muffled cries. My father's low, guttural curses: *Bitch. Whore. Cunt.*

I crept back up the stairs, the sounds of their lovemaking sickening me. My father had done what she asked with the dog and now he wanted sex and she wouldn't give it to him. I was pretty sure this was what was going on. I couldn't help but entertain the sickening notion that I was overhearing the night of my conception all over again.

On my way to my bedroom, I passed by the kitchen and saw the dog collar, still there on the table.

What was happening to us?

SIXTEEN

THE MOHAWK TRAIL was originally a footpath used by Native Americans to walk from what is now Boston to Upstate New York. Today it's paved and carries buses packed with tourists, peering out the windows at the fall leaves. The highway winds through the mountains and is peppered with motels, fruit stands, and maple syrup houses, thick smoke pumping endlessly from their chimneys. There are tacky gift shops all along the trail, and one of them has a giant fiberglass Indian standing guard in front. He must have been twenty feet tall. And not once had we driven past him when I did not whine for my parents to stop.

On this day, though, my mother couldn't stop because she was in a hurry. "We just don't have time. After we pick up my cards in Greenfield, we have to head straight home because I'm meeting Gayle at five."

My mother had sketched an image of a boy in a corduroy coat standing in front of a maple tree, lifting the lid on a bucket attached to the tree and peering at the sap inside. The boy was me and she'd found a local printer to turn the pen-and-ink illustration into note cards. She would pack twelve cards with envelopes into plastic sandwich bags and affix a round white sticker on which she wrote in pencil, "$3.99." Already, the Jeffrey Amherst Bookshop had told her they would carry the cards—her Emily Dickinson series had sold nicely.

Greenfield was about forty minutes from our house. There was something depressing about the town, with so many of its Main Street stores empty, FOR RENT signs taped crookedly in the windows. But I liked Greenfield because its bones were grand. Main Street was wide and elegant. Homes in the town had rolling grass lawns, neoclassical columns, and old fruit trees in front. Greenfield reminded me of a beautiful grandmother that nobody ever visited, but she kept squares of lace on the arms of her sofa anyway.

There was not one interesting thing about the printing shop. A receptionist took my mother's receipt, told us she'd be only a few minutes, and stepped into the back. Restaurant menus, violation notices, and annual reports were hung on the wall and there was a row of hard plastic seats beneath them. There *was* a gumball machine, but it was that handicapped gum, with a picture of a child in crutches attached to the glass ball. It was only a penny and I was pretty sure you'd get more than one piece, but I also figured it would be stale and I'd end up spitting the squares of crackle-coated gum into the trash can, so I just sat down and watched the wall.

After ten torturous minutes, the receptionist reappeared carrying a long blue box with one of my mother's cards taped to the front.

"This looks wonderful, oh I'm just delighted," my mother said, examining the card. "What do you think?" she asked me.

I loved the card. She'd drawn me from a photograph and her drawing looked just like the picture. It was neat to think that all these people, strangers, would buy me and send me to their friends. "I like it," I told her.

She paid by check and we left. As we were driving out of town, a storefront caught my eye. "Quick, stop!" I shouted.

"What! What is it?" she cried, jerking the car over to the curb and slamming on the brakes. She looked left, then right to make sure she hadn't hit a dog, a bicyclist.

I pointed to a small bookshop, the window filled with crosses, plastic statues of Jesus and Mary Magdalene. A religious bookstore. My mother was puzzled. "Augusten, why on earth did you make me stop for this store?"

"I don't know," I said. Had the glint of a gold cross caught my eye? Had my eye been drawn to the deep, royal blue of the sky in a painting of Jesus? "All of a sudden, it just seemed like we had to stop," I told her honestly.

My mother had pulled blindly over, but the car had landed at a meter. There was parallel parking all along the street and almost no other cars. "Well, we can run in for a second," she said, checking her watch. "If you really want to."

I didn't really want to now that I saw what it was, but since I'd made her stop I said, "Okay, let's go inside."

She didn't bother putting anything in the meter. It wasn't like there was any competition for the space.

A bell attached to the door jangled when we opened it and the tinkling made me happy because it made the store seem quaint.

I scanned the little shop, but there was nothing there for me.

Just counters filled with small statues, rows of Bibles, framed prints of the Last Supper, the Crucifixion, the Parting of the Red Sea.

But in the back was a glass display case and I walked directly there. The case was filled with jewelry: rings and bracelets, necklaces and pins.

My eye had already landed on a small silver cross. There was a slight flair at the base of the cross, and the silver had a grain, as if somebody had pressed the cross against a grass mat. It hung from a dainty silver chain.

"Mom, I have to have this," I said as she approached me. "I really need it. I'll buy it myself, if you give me an advance on my allowance."

My mother leaned forward. "What do you need? That little cross right there? Augusten, why do you need that?"

"I don't know," I told her. And I didn't. Why was I so drawn to it? Yes, I liked jewelry. Digital watches with black faces, mood rings. But this cross wasn't even shiny and it wasn't gold and it didn't have an embedded gemstone. "I just know I need it."

My mother studied my face for a moment, then she looked back at the cross. A white paper tag dangled from its chain. Nine dollars. "Okay," she said. "We'll get you the cross if you really need it."

The saleswoman was in her late sixties, bony with no extra flesh to spare. Her smile was tight, withholding, and her eyes darted between me and my mother. It must have made her suspicious to see a young man pestering his mother for a little girl's catechism cross. Still, she opened the glass cabinet and hooked the silver chain over her nail, lifting it out. "This is what you'd like to see?" she asked.

"No, that's okay," I said. "We'll take it. You can just wrap it up please."

She smiled her tight smile and said, "Very well." She laid it on a sheet of white tissue paper, folded, and folded again. Then she taped the edges and handed me the package.

My mother paid and we left. This time, I didn't even hear the bell I was so strangely excited.

Once inside the car, I tore the tissue paper open, shook the cross out in my hand. I opened the clasp and placed the chain around my neck. I borrowed the rearview mirror to see that the cross dangled just below the hollow of my neck. It was tiny, a first piece of jewelry for a little Catholic girl. I didn't care.

Being given a dollhouse a few years back had fortified me against such trivial mortifications.

THE NEXT MORNING I folded the backseat of the wagon flat and helped my father load the car with green trash bags for a trip to the dump. My mother had mentioned that she might come, too, so I kept the front seat clear of bags so the three of us could squeeze in together.

Once the car was packed, my father climbed in behind the wheel and pulled the car forward to the middle of the driveway. I ran up alongside and when he stopped I opened the passenger-side door. "Wait," I said, "I think my mother's coming." Then I climbed in and slid to the center of the bench seat, leaving the door open for her.

We waited. I craned my neck to look back at the house, waiting for her to appear. Finally, the screen door opened and my mother stood in the doorway.

I would have grinned at her. I would have scooted over to

the edge of the seat, leaned out and waved. I would have called to her, "Hurry!" But I did none of these things because in an instant, my father suddenly exploded.

His hands clamped down on the steering wheel.

His knuckles, bone-white against the raw, scaling, furious red of his gripping fingers.

I saw his face in profile, the blood-filled purple color of internal organs; a spleen, the interior of a stomach. His teeth were a cage, two rows of a grimace, cracking together. *Klack, klack.* No tongue.

His head swiveled on the stalk of his neck, cords in his throat tightened like cables beneath the skin. The whites of his eyes were more yellow than white, webbed with red veins finer than hairs. The eyes bore into me and from the pit of his body he growled.

He threw the car into drive and I hit the back of the seat as his foot crushed the gas.

The door bounced and slammed shut. I turned in my seat and saw my mother standing on the front steps, the telephone receiver stretched all the way from the kitchen, falling from her hands, her mouth in a horrified *O*.

Gravel exploded against the underside of the car. When we hit the end of the driveway, he didn't stop; he turned left and stomped on the gas like he was trying to stomp a rat. I screamed for him to stop. "Stop!"

But he snarled or barked—an ugly noise that human people never make—and the car roared forward, rear wheels fishtailing, the engine making a horrendous whine.

Crouched against the door, away, as far away from him as I could get, I looked at his face but his gaze was fixed. I followed his sight line out the window and saw the pond and just beyond it: a telephone pole.

He was steering for the pole.

Now, I turned my body in the opposite direction and hooked my fingers under the door handle. I pulled and the door opened.

I leaped out of the car.

I landed hard on the packed dirt, rolled, rolled again, sticks cracked beneath my back and I bounced against the embankment. Stillness. And then *up*. I had to get up.

Not hurt, fast, I ran. I ran home.

My lungs were too small, too hot, it felt like they were melting in my chest. At the bottom of our driveway, I saw home. My mother, she was there, she was running, she was calling my name, "Augusten, *Augusten*." And hearing my name, hearing *her voice* call my name made me know I was alive but it terrified me, too, because it turned what just happened into something true that I could never wipe away. Hearing her call my name, seeing her run for me, was the same as light striking film.

I was in her arms. She was strong, wrapped around me. And then we were running up the driveway. Together.

Inside the house we separated. There was no speaking, we just knew. She ran downstairs to her bedroom; I ran to mine. I gathered what I could carry and ran back out of the house. She had done the same thing. She opened the hatchback and we threw it all in together.

I climbed into her red Vega, reached for the door to slam it shut.

"No," she ordered, "you get in the back." No fear in her voice. Nothing vague.

I hopped back out, folded the seat forward, and climbed in. For a moment we sat parked in a cut-out perpendicular to the driveway. After just a moment, through the windshield I saw my father as he walked toward the driveway from the road. What had happened? Had he crashed the car?

"Lie down," my mother said.

"I don't want—"

"Down!" she screamed and I obeyed.

She stepped on the gas and I rose. I sat up and looked. I had to.

My father was frozen in place, car versus man. My mother rolled down her window and leaned her head out. *"Get out of the way."*

My father remained standing exactly where he was.

My mother stepped on the gas.

I knew only this: My mother would not stop the car and she would not swerve around him. I let the sudden forward momentum throw me to the floor. I didn't want to see.

At the last instant, my father stepped out of the way because suddenly we were on the road. We were driving.

I was shaking uncontrollably. I was saying, "He wouldn't stop. He was so mad, and he was going so fast and I knew he was going to crash us into something."

"I saw," she said simply. "I screamed for you and then I ran after you."

"What happens now?" I asked.

"We're never going back," she said.

And then she said it again. "It's okay. We're never going back."

I touched the silver cross that hung from my neck.

WE CHECKED INTO a Howard Johnson's motor lodge. My mother paid in cash and used an alias, Louisa Ledford. She locked the door, then put on the chain. We dragged the heavy, vinyl-backed drapes closed. We didn't turn on any lamps. The only light in the room came from the television, which I watched muted.

After this, we stayed a few nights with one of my mother's friends and her family. Even though my mother and I were together, I'd never felt so distant from her. It was as if *she* was on the run and I had just come along, like her pocketbook. Except she never let her pocketbook out of her sight. I knew, somehow, that I was losing her, that she was already gone. Her eyes frightened me, there was too much white. Her breath was all wrong. She was too *animal*. Something was wrong with her mind.

The construction of my world was failing.

We went to her psychiatrist's house and sat in the front room and when a car passed by, we ducked out of sight. Her doctor announced that my father was homicidal. And when I heard this, something in my head *clicked*. It was a mechanical sensation, like one gear fitting into another. And then it was as if a small amount of pressure were relieved, a blister popped. Because now I had a name for what it was about my father that had always puzzled me, always been on the tip of my tongue and yet impossible to quite say. Before, I'd explained to myself that he was missing something. Or there was something *off* about him. But now I had the word for it.

WHEN WE PULLED into the driveway a few days later and saw my father's shadow behind the screen door, my mother said, "Damn it to hell, he's supposed to be gone." She killed the engine, and we sat for a moment.

I saw his dark form standing behind the screen door. A trick of the light made him appear as not a man in shadow, but the black *absence* of a man, a cutout, a void. "We are not safe here," I said to my mother.

"It's okay. He won't hurt us. This will be very quick."

I climbed out of the car and Cream did not run to me. My precious, joyful Ice Cream, just a massive puppy at heart. I called her name and heard her bark. I followed the sound of her voice and discovered her back in the woods, tied to a tree. No water bowl, no food. As I approached, she leaped at me, choking on her cruel leash, wild with excitement and relief.

If we hadn't come home to get clothes that day, Cream would be dead. And what would my father have done, then? Put her head on a stick and placed it at the foot of the driveway, to welcome us when we did finally come?

If I turned out to be anything like him when I grew up, I would destroy myself. I unleashed Cream and led her to the spigot. I cupped my hands beneath the flow and offered her my human bowl.

I would not go inside the house. My mother packed for me.

WE MOVED INTO the basement unit of an apartment house in Amherst. A local priest had made the arrangements. Nobody knew our address, it was a secret. Cream came with us.

Every time I stepped outside, I looked all around me in every direction before venturing forward. The sun was merely a bother, illumination when I needed darkness and the safety of concealing shadow.

In bed at night, I could not take my eyes off the window across from my bed, terrified I would see his face suddenly be-

hind the black glass. That he never appeared hardly mattered—
the window owned me nonetheless. My eyes belonged only to
it and I was tired, so tired.

"Why aren't you sleeping?" my mother asked, noticing the
dark crescents beneath my eyes.

"I'm scared," I said. I refused to say why. I wouldn't tell her
that I spent my nights watching the window, expectantly. I worried that to voice the fear might make it become true. I could
possibly create the fact of him outside my window just by
speaking the words.

MY FATHER MOVED out of the house and my mother and I
moved back in. He rented a single room in the cellar of a house
on Lincoln Street, in downtown Amherst.

My mother could not bear to be in the house she'd shared
with my father, even though now it was just the two of us. She
gave a few poetry readings. She saw her psychiatrist. She called
a real estate agent to put the house on the market. The agent
walked through the rooms and I saw the house through her eyes:
the filthy, worn floors, the rotten deck, neglect everywhere.

With my mother gone most of the time, the house was
mine. I cracked a tooth eating dry spaghetti from the box.

One day my mother told me, "I'll be home late tonight."

It was dark. She'd been gone for hours. The phone rang. I
picked up the wall phone in the kitchen. "Hello?"

It was my father. "Son?" He was drunk. I could hear it in
that one word.

"Yeah?" I said, walking with the phone attached to my ear
out into the hallway. It was a long cord and stretched all the way
to the front door.

"Son?"

"Yeah?"

"I have stolen a car. It's a Mustang. And I am driving out there to the house right now and I'm going to kill you." There was silence. And I heard him breathing.

"What did you say?" I whispered.

The phone went dead.

I let go of the receiver. Because I'd stretched the cord to its limit standing near the front door, the phone flew back into the kitchen and smashed against framed photographs on the wall.

I ran into the kitchen, did not see the shattered glass, and stepped all over the shards. My feet began to bleed immediately, the blood making the floor slippery. I lost my balance, slid, then brought my other foot down hard to catch myself, and sliced my toes.

I hurried out of the kitchen, running straight for the front door. I locked it. When I turned around, I was surprised to see my own bloody footprints on the floor. I looked down and saw that my feet were covered with blood. And I wondered if I had lost too much already.

I ran back into the kitchen, sliding along the way, and hung up the phone.

Where was my mother? Could I call her? I could not.

I dialed *4* on the rotary phone, screaming "Come on, hurry" as the dial slowly returned to its neutral position. I dialed, *1* and then *1* again. "God, hurry, come on, ring, ring, ring." I was frantic, my heart pounding, my feet pounding as if they each contained their own beating heart. I endured three, four rings, and then the operator picked up. I asked for the number for the Amherst police department. And then I dialed it very carefully, so that I didn't make a mistake and have to start over.

In the middle of the number I realized I should have just called 911 but it was too late now, I couldn't start over.

The police answered immediately.

There was too much breath behind my words and I couldn't focus. "My father just called saying he stole a car and is coming out to kill me, it's a Mustang he said and he isn't far, he could be at the reservoir by now and there's so much glass here, it's easy to get in."

The officer may have asked me questions and if he did, I answered them. He may have given me instructions and if he did, I followed them. I remember nothing until fifteen minutes later when the phone rang again and I answered.

It was an officer. His tone surprised me, the anger in his voice. "We're here at your father's apartment and he's not drunk. He's not stolen any car. He seems perfectly fine. You know, this is a very serious thing you've done, this prank."

"Put my father on the phone," I snapped.

I waited.

"Hello, son?" my father said, sounding concerned. "What's going on here, what have you done?" His voice was bone-dry sober.

"Why?" I asked him. "Just *why*?"

"Why what, son? Are you upset? Are you all right?"

"You just called me, drunk. You said you'd stolen a car, you said you'd stolen a Mustang and were coming out here to kill me. What's going . . . why are you . . . this is . . ." I couldn't get the words out, fury and terror and confusion overwhelmed me. I was standing in my own blood.

"Son, I did not just call you," he insisted. And I would have believed him, fully, had I not just spoken to him moments before. For one brief, dark instant I questioned myself.

An officer came back on the line. "We even checked under the bed," he said. "We didn't find anything, not so much as an empty bottle. What kind of game are you playing here?"

He waited for my answer.

And when I didn't give him one he continued, "Don't you ever do that again. Calling the police like this? Wasting everybody's time? Don't you *ever*." Finally, he said, "This is a lousy thing to do to your own father, kid."

Then he hung up on me.

I STOOD EXACTLY where I was beside the wall phone and my chest convulsed as the sobs came out of me in rolling waves. Tears dripped from my eyes and a long strand of mucus hung from the tip of my nose and I felt something washing out of me.

My mother came home and found me sitting in the dark kitchen, dried blood and glass still on the floor at my feet. When she saw me, she froze. "My God," she whimpered. "Oh my God, what has happened?" Her breath smelled like coffee and this trace of normalcy restored my ability to blink and breathe and exit my stupor.

As I recounted the details of what happened, I never once took my eyes off hers because I needed her to hear every word I said and I needed her to believe me.

And because this was the man that she married, the father of her children, the one she knew so well, she did.

THE FURNITURE FROM our home in Shutesbury was now crammed into a much smaller rental house in Amherst. It was strange to see the black metal bookcases that had once lined the expansive rear wall of my parents' bedroom now assembled in the living room, blocking the two windows. The long floral sofa, which at home had floated on a white rug in front of the sliding glass doors, now ran the length of the living room wall. Everything I'd grown up with was here, mashed into these few rooms.

The divorce itself was just a piece of paper signed by a judge and yet it had a profound impact on my mother. It was as if her entire personality changed. There was something wild in her eyes, fierce and furious. She paced the apartment like a caged animal and struggled for weeks with the same seventy-line poem. She called it, "my masterpiece."

She was under the care of her psychiatrist, a white-haired Svengali who had a group of loyal patients, or followers, many of whom tithed ten percent of their incomes to him. The doctor had a large biological family and a number of extended family members—a "spiritual brother," additional "wives," and "adopted" children, many of whom were his psychiatric patients.

I began spending time at the doctor's run-down, rambling house in Northampton. There was always somebody there, something going on. And it was better than being cooped up in the small Amherst home with my mother.

In time, I would move into the doctor's home with his family. I would be given my own room, which I would paint white with bright red trim. The doctor would become my legal guardian.

And my mother would struggle through multiple psychotic episodes, tended to by the doctor and her new girlfriend, at eighteen just a few years older than me. She was also one of his patients.

These years living with the doctor and his family would come to be the defining years of my life.

And when I finally broke free, it would be many years before I fully comprehended just what had happened.

SEVENTEEN

ONCE, HOLYOKE, MASSACHUSETTS, was a thriving industrial city on the banks of the Connecticut River. Settled originally in the early seventeenth century by Englishmen, Holyoke's very bones are British. Stand beside one of the old brick paper factories—its tapered, elegant smokestack reaching high into the sky—and squint, and you'd swear you were looking back in time at a factory along the River Thames. In the residential areas, wide boulevards are lined with old-growth oak and elm trees and the mansions are set back from the street—Greek revival, Victorian, Tudor. These were the homes of the paper factory owners and managers. Glorious, stately structures decidedly European in their design and construction.

In 1919, even Rolls-Royce opened a manufacturing plant in Springfield, the city next to Holyoke. The plant was a brilliant success, producing over three thousand Rolls-Royce motor cars. But in 1929, the Great Depression forced the plant to close forever.

Yet, Springfield remains the only location outside of the United Kingdom where Rolls-Royce cars were ever made.

Dr. Seuss was born in Springfield and was a teenager when Rolls-Royce opened its doors there.

Holyoke could have become another Boston, or even a New York City, but instead, it stopped following the bread crumbs and lost its way. After the war, when the American economy moved away from manufacturing, Holyoke failed to reinvent itself. It just sat there and wondered where everybody went. And then it began to smell bad and its wounds became infected and it stopped bathing.

The city plunged into failure. It became the grimmest, poorest city in Massachusetts. A splotch of cancer in the center of the state. An entire brick factory, weeds sprouting from between the mortar, could be bought for tens of thousands of dollars. You could buy yourself a Craftsman home right near the river for under ten grand. But then, you'd have to live in it.

The crumbling brownstones that lined the downtown area, once so elegant they could've been in London's Hyde Park or Boston's Beacon Hill, were now in shambles. Some were occupied by check-cashing stands, the clerk seated behind a thick piece of bulletproof glass. Others were repurposed into low-income housing. Slumlords bought entire city blocks and carved up the buildings, cramming in as many families as possible.

The citizens of Holyoke no longer packed tin lunchboxes and went to work at the paper mills or the glamorous Rolls-Royce factory, where only one hide in five hundred was fine enough to become a car's upholstery; many didn't work anywhere. Holyoke was now just another depressed former mill town in a sorry state of decay. The city's greatest resource was its rich Puerto Rican community, with the largest percentage of

Puerto Ricans found in any city in America—second only to
Puerto Rico itself. But like the empty factories and the intricate
canal system, the rich heritage of its people was neglected.
Poverty had infected Holyoke like a virus immune to treatment.

In 1983, at the age of seventeen, I moved into my first apartment on Appleton Street in downtown Holyoke. By lying about
my age and adding a year, I was able to find work as a waiter. And
I was able to afford this, my first apartment. My building had
most of its windows, unlike the surrounding structures, where
the blown-out windows were either boarded up or left as gap-
ing black holes. My street looked like a mouth that had been
punched, knocking out its teeth.

A car, stripped of all its saleable parts, sat outside my apartment building, its charred remains like the bones of a long-dead
animal abandoned on the plains. Graffiti adorned nearly every
building and the murder rate was high enough that you really
had to think carefully before you walked outside to buy a soda,
even in the afternoon.

I had left my mother's psychiatrist's house and was now truly
on my own. After paying my security deposit along with first
and last months' rent, I had seven dollars to last me the week. I
was home now.

The trouble was, I couldn't afford food. At the restaurant, we
were allowed only one small meal from a limited menu. But at
seventeen, I was constantly hungry. It seemed to me I hadn't felt
full since I was twelve, before my parents split apart. Even my
teeth were chipped and cracked. I wasn't getting enough nutrition
to build a whole, complete human body, so my system did the best
it could. Teeth, bones, skin—these, on me, were improvised.

Shortly after moving in, I realized I had to call my father and
ask him to bring me some food. My brother, I knew, wouldn't

do it. He was unreliable and I could never get him to agree to
anything. My mother was too crazy to call. That left my father.
I paced my apartment and tried to think of what I would say.
Dad? It's me. I have my own apartment now, but I'm out of money.
No, that would only generate a lecture about fiscal responsibil-
ity. I thought I could just tell him, *I'm out of food,* and leave it at
that. The more I thought about it, the more that seemed to be
the thing to say. But could we have a normal conversation?
Could I call him and ask him for food and would he bring it?
Could anything be that simple?

At last, I picked up my telephone and dialed his number.
While the phone rang, I steadied my breathing and cleared my
throat. When he answered, I said simply, "Can you bring me
some food? Just to last until I get my next paycheck, in four or
five days."

There was silence on the line. He was considering my re-
quest. Because he hadn't refused automatically, I felt buoyed. I
didn't dare breathe. I could allow nothing to spoil the moment,
ruin the outcome. I stared up at the plaster peeling away from
the light fixture mounted in the center of the ceiling and said a
superstitious prayer, *Please say yes, please just say* yes. I weighed
only 120 pounds, the thinnest I had been since reaching my
adult height of six one.

My fingernails were soft.

Oh, please say yes, you old bastard.

I could almost taste the peanut butter. What would I make
first? A ham sandwich? Or maybe, I could boil water and make
pasta, right on my own stove. With tomato sauce and garlic
bread and . . .

"All right," he said finally. Two words and I would eat. I was
so flooded with gratitude that I couldn't speak. I coughed to

clear my throat. "Thanks," I said, simply. "This is going to help a lot. And I promise I won't call you all the time and ask for food. It's just hard right now, until I can find a second job or arrange for some more hours at work. He said he might be able to do it," I added, referring to my boss, who had blithely replied that he might be able to "scrounge up a few extra hours a week" for me. Even just ten extra dollars a week would make a huge difference.

My father didn't want to hear my gratitude. "Okay, son. That's all right, that's fine now. I have to go. But I'll bring you some food."

I hung up and looked around at the apartment. How would it appear to his eyes? I saw the dingy, yellowed walls, the filthy, nearly opaque window. The floorboards could use a refinishing but there was nothing to be done about that. I had a broom and I used it to sweep up any dust and fallen paint chips that had gathered. I did not have a dustpan, so I swept the debris onto an envelope and dropped it into the trash. I made my bed. And there wasn't much else I could do. I wished I had some flowers or a plant. I wished I had some curtains.

I sat at the chair in front of my typewriter, but I was too anxious to sit still. So I paced some more.

Three hours later, there was a knock on my door. When I opened it, my father handed me a surprisingly small bag, which I brought into my kitchen, set on top of the stove, and began to unpack.

"Well, so," my father said, scanning the surroundings. "Your first apartment, how about that," he chuckled. "Yes sir, your very first apartment. Well, that's very exciting."

I stood motionless, looking at the contents of the bag, which I had now placed on the counter before me.

1. A half-size loaf of Wonder Bread with a red sticker on the wrapper that read, DAY OLD ½ PRICE.

2. One package of Oscar Mayer bologna containing five slices.

3. One can of orange-flavored Hi-C fruit punch with a dent on the side so large that the can was, mathematically, no longer a cylinder.

And that was it.

My heart was pounding in my chest and my eyes stung with tears but I refused to cry in front of him. I would not do that. I said instead, "Thanks for bringing these things," and I smiled.

"Well," he said, "I don't know what you're going to do if you can't afford food. You better not lose this job of yours. I don't—" He stopped speaking and gave up, so discouraged by my pitiful life. He shook his head in disappointment. And at last, he looked me in the eyes. "I don't know what to say to you."

I wanted to spit in his face. I wanted to pour gas on him and light a match. I said, "I'll see you later, then."

He left. I listened to his footfalls on the steps, slow, somber, pained.

I watched from my window as he opened the door, climbed behind the wheel, and drove away in his blue Oldsmobile.

My hatred, the boiling oil rage I felt, had a color: white.

There is anger so powerful that the fist *must* go through the wall. It is not humanly possible to contain or manage this kind of anger.

Yet there is a kind of anger that goes beyond even this. Where you are lifted so high by your fury that for an instant you hover, suspended; the fist does *not* go through the wall. You hold your breath and wait, you hang, you float. This is where I found myself and I *laughed.*

And I continued to laugh.

Standing near my window overlooking the street, I doubled over, my abdominal muscles contracted in hilarity.

Newton's Third Law engaged. Newton's Third Law states: *Forces always occur in pairs. If object* A *exerts a force* F *on object* B*, then object* B *exerts an equal and opposite force* −F *on object* A. Phrased another way: *Every action has an equal and opposite reaction.*

Tears nearly blinded me, liquefying the world outside my window. My cheeks were wet, my nose was running. I was gasping for air, laughter now exploding out of me.

It wasn't food my father brought me.

It was rocket fuel.

I was going to make something of myself. Something *big.*

My laughter was merely the eruption that occurs directly after ignition, as liquid oxygen and liquid hydrogen are converted into directed kinetic energy.

Five, four, three, two, one.

Blast off.

EIGHTEEN

THE WAY I woke from sleep, suddenly, thickly, my dream was still stuck to me. Like a dry tongue, pasted to the roof of a mouth. I was thirty but felt fifty. Even with the blinds closed, as they always were, sunlight bled through the slats and washed the contents of my tiny Manhattan studio apartment. The protective, concealing layer of darkness had been peeled away by the sun and everything looked raw, exposed, like the skin that is revealed when a scab is pulled away. Hundreds of magazines, crumpled and stepped on, pasted to the floor through years of trampling, along with mounds of clothes on the sofa, half-empty Chinese food containers, Evian bottles stuffed with cigarette butts, and empty green Tsingtao beer bottles, many filled with urine. There was a path through the debris from the front door to my desk; from the desk to the bed; from the bed to the bathroom. At night when I drank, the room melted away, became a kind of nest. But in the daylight the room was madness and as I looked around at where I lived, I wondered if what I saw around me was a reflection, the externalization, of what was in my head.

I'd had another one of the dreams.

My left shoulder was numb and I couldn't feel my fingers—I hadn't changed position once all night. I sat up in bed, fully drained, as exhausted as if I'd been running. The sheet and comforter were twisted together into a sort of rope and my legs were intertwined with it. I'd never changed these sheets and had wet the bed again. I knew that by evening, they would be dry once again, but I could not stand to sit in the wet, terrible bed.

I swung my legs over the side and sat, feeling dizzy.

In this dream, I don't know how I killed the person, but I was keeping their body beneath the floorboards. I was living in a different apartment, an old room with wide wood floorboards. I'd peeled up two of the boards and rested the body inside. What was so terrible was that in the dream I was aware that I had been having reccurring dreams where I killed people and had to dispose of the bodies, but this time, I'd really done it. In the dream, I'd woken up hungover and seen the pried-open floorboards. I'd approached the body and felt squeamish, repulsed. I'd wrapped the body in plastic wrap and tape and then a sheet. So in the dream, I was aware that I was having these dreams, and this made it especially real.

I walked from the bed and went into the bathroom. My urine was deep, deep yellow and as I pissed, I tried to aim the stream at the crusty, beige film of scum that encircled the inside of the bowl, to clean it. I'd never scrubbed the toilet.

The dreams were upsetting me. More and more, I was having the same dream. The circumstances were always different but in each, I killed somebody and then had to hide the body or find a way to get rid of it. When I woke up from one of these dreams, I was flooded with relief. I thanked God it was just a dream.

I was concerned, though I mentioned it to no one.

I climbed into the shower and as the hot water sprayed me, I felt the relief of distance from the dream. It was no longer clinging to me, the details so vivid and true. It was beginning to curl up and whither; soon it would evaporate away entirely.

But even then, I would still be left with my problem.

I dried myself by using my hand as a squeegee, sliding it quickly down my arm, legs, chest. I walked through to the main room of the apartment and picked through my laundry bag, the paper receipt still pinned to the side, to search for clean clothes. Jeans, a vintage T-shirt from a tackle shop in New Orleans, clean white socks.

I slung my backpack over my shoulder and left the apartment. Outside, I hailed a taxi and went to my office uptown.

I WAS AN associate creative director at an ad agency in Manhattan. At the office, I was funny and people seemed to like me. I'd worked with the same art director for many years and we traveled together from agency to agency as a creative team, so she assumed she knew me well. A few times a day I would go into the men's room, close myself inside a stall, sit on the toilet, and block my ears with my hands. I would stay that way for a few minutes, trying to calm myself. I had the feeling that my home life, my real life, my dirty life, was leaking out, showing through. I had the feeling that people at the office could see something rotten and disturbing and insane poking through me.

It was essential that my work life remain good and clean and separate from the life that happened after work. Never would it occur to me to make a friend at the office.

I had a few suits, which I wore when it was important to wear a suit. But mostly, I wore jeans and T-shirts.

I worked out six days a week and was proud of my body. It was, for me, another point of difference between me and my father. It was important that I have as many of these as possible.

I dated. But nothing ever became serious because at a certain point, you have to invite the other person over to your apartment and I could never do this.

I had a few male friends, all of whom I'd dated in the past, and I kept them separate from one another. None of my friends had ever met.

I made very good money and spent all of it, every week. I lived paycheck to paycheck and after working in advertising since the age of nineteen, had saved around two hundred dollars.

My goal each day was to get through the day as fast as possible. I worked fast because I wanted to be done. I wanted to be done because I wanted to go home to my nest and drink.

I used to go out to bars. I used to go to clubs. Now, I drank alone. Once drunk, I might wander the streets and look for drugs. Or go to a bar and talk to a stranger.

I was two people. The sane, funny, advertising me. And the other me, that came out at night. It was a constant struggle to manage the two. And lately, I was becoming very worried about this other person. It appeared that he was growing larger. The daytime me was shrinking. I was leaving the office earlier and earlier each day. It was only a matter of time before I quit entirely and went freelance.

Then, I would be accountable to no one.

This other side of me, this whole other person, even ate

foods I didn't like. Sometimes, I woke up to find an opened tin of smoked oysters on the bed. Once, I woke up in a different town. I was on the floor, beside a sofa. On one end of the sofa, a man who was unfamiliar, on the other a woman I'd never seen. I had no idea where I was or how long it would take me to get back to Manhattan.

But I did get back to Manhattan and went to work as if nothing out of the ordinary had happened. As if I'd stayed home the night before and read a novel.

Nobody who knew me, or saw me on the street, would ever guess that I lived the way I did. That I had to keep my apartment air-conditioned year-round to control the odor. That my apartment wasn't merely filthy but diseased.

I had concerns that something might be wrong with me. That the dreams might be a part of me trying to come out. I was afraid I might be a serial killer.

And I was afraid that I was exactly like my father.

He, too, showed the world one face but wore an entirely different one in private. And was I missing empathy? I thought this might be so.

It wasn't that I had fantasies of killing people. But I was having dreams about it. And I had to admit, I didn't know who I was anymore. Perhaps the dreams *were* fantasies, expressing themselves when I was out of the way.

I read books about serial killers to see if I recognized myself. I was riveted by the gruesome details, repelled and fascinated. After each book I told myself, "That's the last one."

One night, I dreamed I was visiting a mass murderer on death row. There was no table between us, we sat in hard plastic chairs, side by side. As he spoke, I looked into his eyes and realized I understood him on a deeper level than I had ever understood anyone

before. He reached for my hand and said, "We're the same." I had
an explosive orgasm. And woke up. I'd had a wet dream, the first
since I was thirteen.

When I read the curious statistic that many serial killers
owned VW bugs, I felt a slight relief. I had owned, after all, a
VW *Fastback*. Surely, this had to humanize me.

All my life, I'd been afraid of turning into my father. And
now, it looked like that was exactly what had happened. I was an
alcoholic, like him. I had a double life, like him. And now, these
terrible dreams, revealing some darker, more sinister part of me.
The him part. The father part.

SHORTLY AFTER THE divorce my father married a secretary
from the university. She was the exact opposite of my mother—
quiet, shy, even meek when you first met her. They lived on a
secluded mountaintop and kept to themselves.

I remained in touch with my father over the years by phone.
It was my way of keeping tabs, of monitoring his state of mind.
It was like I was peeling back a Band-Aid and checking the
wound to make sure it hadn't become infected.

I called him at least once a week. It reassured me to describe my own life to him and hear, for myself, how unalike
we truly were.

I named the places I had seen, listing them like an airline
employee ticking off destinations: Maui, London, Anguilla, the
Grand Canyon, asking him after every one, "You've never been
there, right?"

I described the interior of a limousine, making sure he understood that I had not ordered it for myself, somebody had
thought to order it for me, believed I belonged there. I

explained the process of filming a commercial, demonstrating my expertise in a complex technical field, speaking faster as I sensed his interest diminish. I told him what it felt like to have Lauren Bacall shake me by the collar and say, "Go back to school, kid." When I hired a housekeeper I called him and told him. And when I bought my first cell phone, the size of a brick, he was my first call.

When these details failed to impress him, I laid myself bare and told him my salary, asking, "That's more than you made at my age, isn't it?" knowing that it was. I was reduced to reciting numerals, my worth dependent upon where, exactly, the decimal was placed among the zeros.

He listened while I recited my small accomplishments. And then he said, "Well, I best be going now, son. These phone calls are expensive."

To my own ear I sounded like a toddler proudly proclaiming, *Today I made a pee. And I made poo. And then I walked outside. And then I found a rock. And then the rock was round and so I kept it. And then I found another rock. Only this one was flat and so I kept it, too. And then tomorrow I am going to paint a horse with real paint and paper and everything!* And it sickened me, but I could not stop and had to come back for more. Each time, it was exactly like it had been when I was a little boy, trying to crawl into his lap. Those arms of his, pushing me away. Nothing had changed, though everything had. I was the waiter on the Titanic running after a guest, *Excuse me, but you forgot your change. Hey! I said, you forgot your change.*

Whatever happened between us had happened a long time ago, I told myself. You made it. You're fine. If there is a hole there, simply walk around it. When he told me, "Well, it was awfully cold here this morning," I responded with an enthusiastic,

"*Really?* How cold?" And all the while I was telling myself, "It's okay, see? You aren't a bit like him. You don't care about the weather. You don't even own an umbrella."

As an adult, my father would call me twice.

As an experiment in my early twenties, I decided not to call him to see what would happen. What happened was, we didn't speak for four years.

I fought the nagging compulsion to hand him a document listing all my accomplishments: moving to San Francisco at eighteen and not knowing a single person there; landing a job in advertising at nineteen on the strength of some ads I wrote on the back of scrap paper; being lured away from San Francisco to New York by none other than Ogilvy & Mather advertising. I wanted to present him the names of all the cities I had seen, along with my starting salary and my much larger salary now, photographs of the famous people I had met, the apartments I had seen. I wanted to show him this data and force him to admit that he was wrong about me. I wanted him to be forced to admit that I had made it, despite him. And that I was not him. Award me a prize, a ribbon he crafts himself and pins to my chest—I felt entitled to these formal recognitions.

MANY TIMES THROUGHOUT the years, I thought back to the street I grew up on. Market Hill Road. Sometimes, looking out the window at the city beneath me, a memory would arise and I ceased seeing the city outside, and would for a moment be a child of seven again.

At night in bed, Brutus beside me, for this was before his defection, I am on my back, awake, dreading school, perhaps. Fantasizing about my adulthood, that beautiful promise of my future. When suddenly, there appears on the ceiling of my bedroom a wash of light. Startled, I look up to the window and see there is a light shining in. It moves quickly, around and around, as if somebody is sending me a signal. The flashlight traces the square frame of my window, it makes a figure eight. Busy signals. If I stand on the bed and look out the window, my face will be illuminated but I will see nothing, so I remain where I am. There is no sound, only this light, so Brutus remains asleep. It is my father outside my window, of this I am sure. After a few minutes, the light is gone, just as suddenly as it had appeared. I lie awake for an hour, maybe two, but it does not return that night.

A few times I searched online for "unsolved murders, western Massachusetts." I found nothing. I searched, "missing students, Amherst." I found nothing.

Always, I am drunk when I perform these searches. It takes alcohol both to unlock the desire to search, and then generate the motivation. Alcohol provides the buffer I would require should I stumble on something curious.

As a little boy, I'd had a dream that my father had taken me to the woods where there was a dead body. He buried it and told me I must never tell. It was the only thing we'd ever done together, father and son, and I promised not to tell. But unlike most dreams, the memory of this one never left me. And sometimes, when I drank, I wasn't altogether sure about one thing: was it just a dream?

Dreams tend to grow transparent with time, they thin out like worn fabric. Dreams fade away to white, but the memory of this "dream" has the quality of true memory, a memory of an event, something actually done. It's been with me for most of my life, this feeling that my father and I share his terrible, buried secret. The only reason I know it's a dream is because it *has* to be a dream.

It bothered me greatly that I did these Internet searches, that I had this question. It bothered me and sometimes I felt angry with myself. A body in the woods, a student taken for personal use and then discarded.

Sober, it was nonsense, a frightened child's comic book fear. Drunk, it seemed something terrible that I witnessed and had made myself forget. A fact that united us, father and son, and kept us apart.

Sober, I knew it couldn't be true.

Drunk, I had a sinking feeling that it was.

Drunk, I looked in the mirror and was startled by how much I resembled him, especially the eyes.

THERE HAD BEEN nothing particularly unusual about that week. I'd gone to work every day, written scripts, watched them be killed for one reason or another, written more scripts. There might have been a print ad or two. I may have looked at a few directors' reels. At the end of every day, I went home and drank. I may have thought about my father once or twice though it would have been a vague, unformed thought, perhaps just an image or memory. But Friday evening, at the end of a wholly unremarkable week, I made a call, one I had made countless times before, that on this ordinary day changed my life.

Before I picked up the phone, I sat at my desk and thought: *I want to stop thinking of him in this way. I am tired of believing he is evil. I am too old for this crap. He was a lousy father. He is not a serial killer. And neither am I.*

While I drank, I wrote some e-mails, read the personal ads, looked at a dirty magazine. Beneath all of these actions, a bedrock of just wanting to be free of him.

Missing students, Amherst.

I picked up the phone, pressed the ON button, and out of nowhere, fully surprising, an idea was there. I set the phone on the table and thought it through. Where had *this* idea come from? But it was brilliant, wasn't it? It was demonically clever and couldn't it actually be my literal key? He would never on his own say the words that would set me free of him. If I could just feel he was only a bad father, he was only flawed, he only didn't care. If I could believe that, I felt, I could move on. But as long as there remained about him something nefarious, as long I harbored these suspicions, I was trapped.

It was a bit of a trick.

Though they had been divorced for nearly two decades, my father continued to pay alimony to my mother, who had never worked in her life. Having survived a stroke and now partially paralyzed, my mother was fully dependent upon her ex-husband for all financial support. The dollar amount had not been revised as the years passed. She was living on an income that a judge determined was acceptable for a single woman of the late 1970s.

Though the amount was still small, my father complained bitterly about this obligation. I had learned over time, one way to keep him on the phone longer was to get him to speak about *her*.

Normally, when I called my father he would say, "Well, I have to be going now," after just a few minutes, five at the most. But I'd discovered that I could engage him by probing. "So, why do you suppose she never tried to become a college professor?"

That was how I kept him on the phone.

On this night, I wanted to hear these words: "Oh, son, that's a terrible thought. What on earth has gotten into you? Jesus Christ, son, are you drunk? That's a terrible, terrible thought. I'm hanging up now." Or any variation herein.

I realized, these were the words that would set me free.

To other people, my father was a nice man. He was a mild man. He may have been an alcoholic when I was young, but he'd been sober now for many years.

I knew the truth. I knew that my father was not a nice man. He was just very good at creating an external identity, a mask to show the world. A mask he never took off anymore. Probably, he understood that if he did take off his mask, he might never get it back on.

I picked up the phone again. Right away he asked about the weather in New York, never all that much different from the weather in western Massachusetts. I told him about the weather in New York. And then I told him about a new AT&T commercial that I would soon have on the air. "Watch for glowing red ears," I said, adding, "it's really not very good, but that's their fault and not mine." He said he'd look for it.

And then I said, "You do know my mother takes a walk on that bridge behind her apartment every night. She goes out there alone."

My mother lived beside the footbridge that spanned the river in her town. She walked the bridge to maintain her strength. She walked the bridge alone at night. She loved the river beneath it, the roiling waterfall just beyond. Many of her later poems were about this bridge, the river, the leaves of the trees along the bank changing colors through the seasons.

I said, my voice lowered to a confidential whisper, "You know, you could be *on* that bridge one night when she's out for her walk. Old people fall every day. What would be so unusual about an old, paralyzed lady falling off the bridge and into the water?"

Unexpectedly, I had to repress a laugh at my outlandish suggestion: Why don't you *kill* her? And I prepared myself for the exasperated tone of voice he would adopt, the same tone of voice he used with me when I was a boy. *Oh, for crying out loud.*

I waited but there was only the sound of his breathing—fast, steady, like an animal or a masturbator.

And then he spoke in a soft, uncommonly low voice, as though taking care not to be overheard. "Well, there are sixteen buildings on either side of that river clustered there just near the bridge. Now, all together, those sixteen buildings—and again, these are only the buildings directly on the water, there are more houses in the hills beyond as well as further upstream—so like I said, those sixteen buildings have a total of one hundred and four windows.

"Now, any one of those hundred and four windows could conceivably have a direct view of that very bridge and the water below it. So at eight o'clock at night when your mother generally takes her walk, how many people might be glancing out the window? Just a glance, that's all it would take. Impossible to say."

At first, I was completely perplexed and said nothing at all. Numbers, figures were echoing in my head. What was he talking about? One hundred and four windows? I thought, *He's misunderstood me. He wasn't even paying attention to what I was saying. He's talking about buildings and windows.*

But by the time I took my next breath I understood what he had said.

First, I felt like I have before in dreams, when falling. It was a plunging sensation, purely physical. The bottom of *me* dropping away. And an undulating nausea overtook me. Immediately, I wanted to deny what I had heard. I wanted to go back in time just ten minutes and change my mind about making this phone call. I wanted this to be untrue.

And I had to say something, just to stall for time.

"Well, yeah. It's just not something you'd want to do any-way," I said dismissively.

"Okay, son, well, I have to go now. It's getting late and these phone calls are expensive." It was what he'd said after every phone conversation we'd ever had. His tone of voice was as if we'd discussed the weather, my new commercial, nothing more at all.

I then became sober.

I had been drunk when I called him but now I was not drunk. I was utterly sober. And I sat in my chair, my computer before me, and I stared at the bright screen. And I was over-whelmed with the desire to sleep.

Delicately, I began to perform an autopsy on the conversa-tion we'd just had. I needed to break it down, line by line, and discover where, precisely, I had misunderstood him. I needed to analyze his words, understand what he had truly been saying. My insane "trick" to get him to say what I wanted had obvi-ously infected and warped my understanding of what he meant.

I lit a cigarette and inhaled the smoke deep into my lungs. So the first question would be, why would my father know how many buildings overlooked the bridge and the river beneath it? How, or why, would he know the exact number of windows?

In order to know these figures, one would have to count. One would have to stand on the bridge and look out at the houses on either side of the banks. And then one would have to count, patiently, carefully. One would write the figure in a small notebook.

Which, as it happened, was something he always carried with him in his pocket. A small notebook. All his life.

And then, make a second count of all the windows. To be sure.

And why would one do this? What other reason could there be for knowing the total number of windows that overlooked the bridge and having these figures available, at a moment's notice, committed to memory?

I flashed back to that night I was alone at the house and he called me. "Son, I've stolen a car and I'm going to drive out there and kill you." As an adult, I'd decided he must have been drunk. He must not have known what he was saying.

And when the police arrived at his house and then phoned to scold me for calling them, when they handed the phone to my father and he spoke without a trace of alcohol in his voice, I'd let this go, too. I'd decided, *I don't need an answer for that.*

Now, sitting in my apartment, I understood something. My father was a careful construction. A studied husk. That's why when he smiled, it was *wrong.* The smile simply unzipped his face to reveal the darkness behind it.

Throughout my childhood I'd seen him sitting in that rocking chair staring at the wall. And what had I thought about that? I suppose, I hadn't thought much. It frightened me, but I didn't know exactly why.

But now, I knew why. Because all that time, he'd been *thinking.*

His mind moving like a muscle.

I put out the cigarette and shoved my chair away from my computer. What, then, had he done with all that rage? Where did all that *other stuff* within him go?

And then I wondered, are there memories missing?

I knew I couldn't remember my father much at all until I was five or six. For me, that's a long time. After all, I could remember the farm in Hadley and I wasn't much older than one. So if pieces of those first six years of him are missing, couldn't there be others also cut out of my mind?

I didn't want to know.

My phone call hadn't set me free. It had made me sick.

I'D RENTED A car one Saturday I returned to Massachusetts. I drove to my old house and saw it was a new color now. It looked smaller. Somebody had replaced the deck. I parked at the end of the driveway and for ten minutes, watched the house as though it might do something—shift position on its lot or flinch. I knew it was the house I had grown up in but it was hard, somehow, to feel this. I was tempted to ring the bell and ask if I could just take a look around inside. But I did not. I had business to take care of.

Then I drove the unfamiliar route to my father's new town. My mother and my father lived in the same town, even after all these years. Divorced for longer than they were married, some bond between them could not be broken. My father lived on his mountain and my mother lived in the village itself, right on the river.

I parked and walked the short distance to the bridge. I walked to the very center and could see my mother's apartment. Buildings lined both sides of the riverbank and I didn't need to count the windows to know how many there were. My father had done that already.

I leaned over the railing and looked at the water below. I stood up and looked toward the end of the bridge on my mother's side. I imagined her walking toward me, a smile of recognition on her face. And then, as she stepped beside me, pushing her over. I closed my eyes and tried to see it in my mind, tried to feel my hands against her shoulders, the thin fabric of her blouse as I pushed. I tried to hear her scream. And then I opened my eyes and I understood something. I knew one thing, and this knowledge was as unique to me as my breath or my fingerprints.

I could never do it.

Not if there were a gun to my head.

And I couldn't push my father off the cliffs of Martha's Vineyard, either. I'd wanted to, once. And I almost had the chance. But I couldn't have done it, not then, not now.

My father hadn't pushed my mother over the bridge. He may have known how many windows were there but he hadn't done anything to her. Could he?

I didn't know. And I probably never would. Part of me wanted to believe my father wasn't a murderer, either. Part of me wanted to believe he'd stood on this same bridge and after counting those windows, understood that he couldn't do it, either.

But in the chambers of my heart, in my very valves, I believed my father was flawed. I believed my father was really not so different from the serial killers I'd read about in all those books. I didn't want this to be true but I felt that it was.

My father and I would never be close. He would never give me what it was I wanted from him. And somehow, I seemed almost all right. I used to believe I couldn't grow up right without a father, that I would never be "normal" without one. But maybe, a father is really a luxury after all. Maybe you could grow up without one.

Another thing was clear to me in this moment: I was not him. I was me. Whatever wrong thing he contained, he had not passed it on.

A breeze blew up off the river, a gust so powerful it knocked me off balance and I stumbled. And I realized, my knee didn't hurt. Not at all. And I wasn't tired. I glanced down, examined my arm. I touched the smooth skin, free of psoriasis, not crusting and peeling, not raw and bleeding, not angry and red, but pale and soft and alive.

I was not my father.

But I wasn't quite myself yet, either.

NINETEEN

Ten years later

THE LARGE DINING room table and eight chairs had been moved out of the room and I wondered briefly where they could be stored. The sideboard was still in place, though it was covered now with the supplies one requires to transport the living into death—hypodermic needles, a plastic rack filled with small glass ampoules, a portable cardiac monitor inside a padded canvas carrying case. A steel-framed hospital bed had been positioned in the dining table's place and in this bed, my father lay, his withered body wasted down to under one hundred pounds. His skin was the color of butter and the whites of his eyes were bright yellow and made me think of a wolf's.

Two months before, my father had fallen backward down his stairs. He'd been taken first to a hospital, then a nursing home for physical therapy. But the medications had been too hard on his liver. Instead of growing stronger in the nursing home, he became weaker, smaller. And now he was dying.

A catheter bag strapped to the side of his bed frame contained only the smallest amount of urine—soon, his kidneys would cease altogether. Maybe in an hour, maybe a day.

The hospice nurse placed a small morphine drip control wand in my father's hand. "When you feel you need more, just push the button right there on the tip. You only need to push it once and you'll get another dose."

Though it was only three in the afternoon it felt much later, because up here on the mountain where my father and his wife had lived for over twenty years, the trees blocked most of the light and the larger mountain behind the house cut the sun off a couple of hours before it set.

My father's wife busied herself in the kitchen, making pitchers of iced tea, wiping the counters with a sponge, brewing coffee. My father's brother and his brother's wife had flown up from Alabama. But my father was too sick for any socializing.

Uncle Bob took a chair in the sunroom, just off the dining room. Aunt Relda had poured him a drink, three fingers of whiskey, and now sat with an iced tea on the sofa. My father's wife had finished up in the kitchen and was now sitting in the recliner opposite Uncle Bob. My brother sat on the sofa beside Relda looking lost and sad. I sat on the floor at Uncle Bob's feet, looking up at him. It was comforting to hear his full, ripe southern accent. It made me realize my father's had been smoothed out over the years, like a stone in a river.

"Now, you have to remember, Marist was the Catholic military school that we attended as boys in Atlanta. And by God, ol' John was battalion commander his senior year there. Buddy?" And here, he looked pointedly at me. "That was no small thing. Battalion commander is *the* top cadet. Your daddy was *the* mutherfucker that got to call quittin' time."

I realized I must have seen photographs of my father in his school uniform, an officer's hat perched on his head. I stood up and walked through the dining room, past my father, who gazed at the ceiling with glassy, unfocused eyes. I jogged up the three steps and walked into his office. I pulled his old photo album from the bottom shelf of his bookcase and carried it back into the dining room. Standing beside his bed, I opened the album to the first page. "I thought maybe you'd like to look at some childhood pictures," I said, holding the album before his eyes.

I imagined that if I were dying it would be a comfort to see, again, my long-dead mother, my distant childhood. But my father simply closed his eyes and rolled his head away from me so that his cheek rested on the pillow. "Well, maybe later," I said.

A few hours later, while I sat in the sunroom listening to Uncle Bob tell more stories, I watched my brother step up to the hospital bed. Gently, he stroked our father's head. I rose from the sofa and entered the dining room, standing back near the foot of the bed.

In a gravelly whisper my father said to my brother, "You've been a good boy. A good son."

And then my father looked at me. For just a moment, our eyes met and I watched as he opened his mouth, as if to beckon me closer. I did step closer and placed my hands on the rail at the foot of his bed. I waited to hear what he was going to say to me.

It was like the pause after a flash of lightning, before the thunder.

He opened his mouth and then I saw a certain resignation in his eyes and the fire in them dimmed, then vanished altogether. He closed his mouth and then his eyes. My father had changed his mind. He had decided that he had, in the end, nothing to say to me.

And I knew somehow these would be his last words. To my brother he had said, "You've been a good boy, a good son." And to me he'd said nothing. He would not, at the very end, give me even one word.

And standing there, I felt a sense of loss. Not for myself but for him. He had missed so much not knowing me. He had denied himself his greatest accomplishment—to just be a dad.

Uncle Bob roared with laughter in the next room. "*All* their kids were cross-eyed and I was scared to death of cross-eyed folks. I would beg John not to make me do it, but he would gleefully have me follow him right past that old house filled with cross-eyed kids. Crazy, I know it, I know it. But I still don't like cross-eyed people—they're spooky!"

For a while, I watched my father sleep. Briefly, he awoke and turned his face toward the window. Though he could see only the room reflected back in the dark glass, he continued to stare. I saw him shiver, then a tiny cry—a whimper—escaped him. He seemed so utterly small. Only the hospice nurse hovered near him; everybody else was in the other room. I wondered, if he'd been a different man, would everyone now be gathered around his bed, photographs scattered on the thin blanket, his favorite music playing on the stereo, laughter in the air, hands touching him? My father was dying alone, just a few feet away from his family.

Later that evening, I left. During the drive home, I thought of my friend George, who had died so many years before. He, too, had wasted to nearly nothing, just a sliver of his former self, but somehow he'd retained every pound, every ounce of his *being*. George had died with his magnitude intact.

In the morning, my father's wife called to tell me my father had died. "There won't be a funeral," she said. "Your father didn't want one."

The boy whose photograph I studied as a child, who was raised by three doting teenage aunts in a small white house in Chickamauga, the boy who had a drugstore all to himself and loved the Andrews Sisters, who went to Catholic military school and studied Latin and became battalion commander, who was a preacher and then a philosopher, who married my mother and terrified me so fully that I could think only of pushing him off a cliff, this man who had tumbled backward down his stairs and never healed, was, at last, dead.

I was free of him.

Two months later, my father's wife gave me a box. This was my inheritance. Inside the box was an old Bible I had often admired because of its fine leather cover, the Timex watch I'd given my father as a child, a few old family photographs, and four diaries.

It took me the better part of a year before I could bring myself to read these journals, written during the worst years of his life with my mother.

Tuesday, May 27, 1975
78°—Mostly cloudy am
60°—Rain late pm

Went by Hastings and got some Venus Velvet #1 pencils for $1.32 a dozen and a world map for $1 to put in the kitchen to go with my radio cards . . . Ford came on tonight to announce another tariff hike on imported oil which will now raise prices of petroleum products even more in this time of financial desperation. Damn heating oil is already 38.9 a gallon. Got a pair of front tires for the Chrysler on sale—cost me $64. Augusten and I went over and shopped around Northampton . . . Didn't buy anything but he wanted a burglar alarm for $2. Felt bad today—sort of pained in the liver area . . .

I remembered that alarm. It was white plastic with a brass-colored chain. I wanted to attach it to my door, but my father explained, "Son, we have hollow-core doors. If you try screwing this into the door it'll just fall right out. Why on earth do you want an alarm, anyway?"

I hadn't told him, *Because of you. Because I don't want to wake up again and find you standing in my room watching me with that look in your eyes and something terrible in your hands.*

I hadn't said anything at all. I'd put the lock back on the shelf and we'd gone home.

I could see now, it wouldn't have mattered. Even if he'd bought me the lock on that day so many years ago, it wouldn't have made a bit of difference. Nothing could have kept me safe from him. There was no place to hide.

Page after page, as his life fell apart all around him, my father wrote down the prices of corn, gasoline, and long-distance telephone calls. A stranger reading the diaries would think: *What an ordinary life.*

What an ordinary man.

Even his personal diaries had been a construction, masking who he really was inside.

Only once did my father reveal a glimpse of his true nature.

On a page all by itself he wrote, "Augusten very distant tonight. Probably because of my games."

EPILOGUE

I AM ON a book tour. In each city I am greeted by a media escort who picks me up at the airport and drives me to radio stations for interviews, the reading venue, back to the hotel in the evening. I am in Boston for two days. My escort's name is Ginny and I'm fond of her. It has been a long tour and the herniated disks in my back have made it difficult.

A number of times I remind myself of my father: as I wince when I lean forward over the baggage claim carousel to pick up my bag; in the morning when I climb out of bed and feel like I've been in a car accident. My father has been dead two years. I expected to feel a wave of grief hit me after he was gone but it never came.

Ginny, though, takes my mind off my back and the fact that it has been almost two months since I have been home and I miss my family. Ginny is a tall, sweating glass of lemonade and as I sit in her car having no idea where I am—the suburbs, somewhere—I am laughing with my head thrown back. The kind of laugh that clenches your stomach and feels, always, over-due and like you will now live a year longer.

At the end of the day, Ginny tells me, "Tomorrow, I have an-other author. I'm going to send my husband to take you to your event at Harvard. I hope that's okay?"

I tell her it's absolutely okay. I look forward to meeting her husband.

She tells me, "He looks like Senator McCain. You can't miss him."

And when he arrives in his fashionably ramshackle 1970s Mercedes sedan, I see that he does, in fact, look remarkably like the senator.

With his oxford shirt, his collegiate blazer, khaki slacks, and navy and red diagonal stripe tie, he is the personification of Preppy Classic. Ruggedly handsome, he welcomes me with a firm handshake and a surprising almost bumbling warmth that takes me a little off guard. "Sorry about my car," he says, swiping up a pile of folders and tossing them in the back. "Everybody tells me I should get rid of it but it still works. No reason to get a new car when this one keeps ticking."

There is a sparkle in his eye and I don't believe him. The real reason he has not traded the old car in for a new one is because this car is the real thing. It's a little disheveled and extremely classy and the man looks good in the car. And this is why he drives it.

I smile. I like the guy.

I don't pay attention as we take off for Cambridge, because I know I will never drive in Boston. Peeling down the streets, he takes sharp corners, just makes a couple of lights, and delivers us to the venue early and with supreme confidence. We park and start walking.

My event is in the bookstore. He opens the door for me and it's always a little embarrassing when another man does this, but I walk through, thanking him. We take the escalator up and realize—wait, we're in the wrong building. The event is next door.

"But you know? I think my son's graduation robe might be here."

We've paused on a virtually empty floor, most of the lights off. An EMPLOYEES ONLY sign blocks our way from entering the room to our right of this landing. I ask, "Robe?"

And he explains that next weekend, his son, Sam, will graduate from Harvard Medical School. "They give them green robes to wear at the ceremony, with their names stitched onto the front. I think they're green. They were last year, I'm pretty sure. Anyway, this is where they store the robes before the ceremony. It should be just in here. But, well, never mind. We should head next door."

He's a little anxious. He keeps glancing over to the darkened room where the robes probably are.

I step around the EMPLOYEES ONLY sign. "Come on," I say. "Let's find the robe."

IT'S A STORAGE room and now it's filled with garment racks. The racks are filled with robes, just like he said.

"Are you sure you don't mind? It'll only take a second," he says.

The fact that he is so humble, and hides so well his intense curiosity and longing, charms me. "Come on," I say. "Let's find his robe."

They are alphabetized so the hunt is brief. We locate the letter of his son's last name. We begin to hunt through the robes. Quickly, he finds the spot where the robe should be. But it's not there. He checks the names of the robes on either side. It's not there, either.

His disappointment is something physical I can feel beside me in the room.

"Oh, I'm sorry about that," I tell him.

He's chipper. He claps his hands together, though there's a glisten in his eyes. "Ah, it's okay, it's no big deal at all. It's nothing. Hey, the ceremony is next week. I don't need to see the robe today, it doesn't matter."

And then, once more, he turns to check the rack. He slides one robe out of the way and checks the name on the robe beside it.

Quickly, I turn my back on him. The top of my head is about to blow off. I gasp once and tears spring to my eyes, fill them. Quickly, I cough, choke down the sob and I wipe my tears fast with my left wrist.

"Yeah, not here. Okay, shall we go, then?" he says.

I felt it.

The love, it was so strong. How can I possibly describe this love? It is a force of nature. It is great, like the dust bowl but wonderful instead of terrible.

The pride this man feels for his son, to graduate from Harvard Medical School, a doctor. The pride, this father's. The love, this father's. For his son. It is completely overpowering.

Never in my life have I felt anything like it.

Of course I know fathers love their sons. I have seen movies. I have watched TV.

I get it.

But until this moment, I have not felt it. And now, I have.

And it is not even mine. It leaked out of somebody else and stained me. It was not intended for me. It is not mine. And yet, I felt it. There was so much of it, so much love, so much adoration, so much of everything that is fine and good and wonderful and *right* with the world inside this man that he could not contain it.

The grief I feel is crushing and as we leave the room, I follow him because my legs are shaking and I know if he were to look at me he would ask, *Are you okay?* and I am not. I am not okay.

Because I can feel what it is I did not have.

I never felt it before.

How can you really miss something when you've never experienced it? The longing is purely academic. It's book knowledge.

But tonight, I felt it. I felt it, I felt it, I felt it.

And, God, what? What would I give to feel it just once, all for me?

As we descend on the escalator I am shaking as I sob silently. I inhale carefully so that I don't make a sound. Tears have sprinkled the lenses of my glasses.

Out on the street, the sun hits us from its low angle and the sky is a fiery orange. Car chrome, earrings on the woman walking past—everything metallic blazes, reflecting the burning color of the sky.

Even though the sky is still bright, I can see the moon and beside it three stars, or are they planets?

I know that behind these three stars, in the darkness that is hidden now by light, are other planets and numberless stars. Whole galaxies, just like ours. Other worlds.

And maybe on one of them, there is another me. And I am

wearing my green robe with my name stitched onto the chest. And I am standing on stage as somebody hands me my diploma and out in the audience, all I can see is the radiance of one man whose eyes are so shining blue they blind me. And he is smiling and weeping and he is my father and he loves me with all the force of the expanding universe. He looks up at me and he mouths the words, "Very much I love you."